BREATHE
AWAY
YOUR TENSION

BY   DR. BRUNO HANS GEBA

ILLUSTRATED BY ROSELYN BABCOCK RICHARDS

A RANDOM HOUSE ✿ BOOKWORKS BOOK

Copyright © 1973 by Bruno Hans Geba

All rights reserved under International and Pan-American Copyright Conventions

First printing: March 1973:   1,500 copies in cloth
                              20,000 copies in paperback

Illustrated by Roselyn Richards
Cover design by Anne Kent Rush
Typeset by Vera Allen Composition Service, Hayward, California
        (special thanks to Vera, Dorothy, Betty and Gary)
Printed and bound by
under the direction of Stevan Baron and Peggy de Ugarte, Random House
Art Editor: Anne Kent Rush
Cover photographs by John Pearson

This book is co-published by   Random House Inc.
                              201 East 50th Street
                              New York, N.Y. 10022

                      and   The Bookworks
                              1409 Fifth Street
                              Berkeley, California 94710

Distributed in the United States by Random House, and simultaneously
published in Canada by Random House of Canada Limited, Toronto

The publishers wish to thank the following persons for permission to use
their photographs: Suzanne Geba, Reynaldo Cortez, Morris Gustin, Jean Porter.

Library of Congress Cataloging in Publication Data

Geba, Bruno Hans, 1927-
        Breathe Away your Tension

        1.   Mental hygiene.   2.   Mind and body.
3.   Breathing exercises.   I.   Title.
RA782.B7   615.'836   72-12613
ISBN 0-394-48468-1
ISBN 0-394-70972-1 (pbk)

Manufactured in the United States of America

TABLE OF CONTENTS

to SUZANNE

INTRODUCTION

I am Bruno. In this book I will talk to you about your **awareness** (where your head is) and your **body** (where you are). Your body can only be in the present. It is at every moment of your life a part of that very moment. Every breath you take, you take here and now. Your body IS. The place is here; the time is now. It is different with your awareness. During most of your life, your awareness is not in the present. Either you anticipate what might happen or you reminisce about what should have happened. Your head is in the future or in the past. You worry today about tomorrow. "If I don't pass the examination, I won't get the job." Or you lose Thursday anticipating Friday. "I can hardly wait until Friday when we'll be together again." The same is true about the past. "I should have told him off." "Why didn't I ask her when I had the chance?" "How could he do this to me?" "Things sure were great back in Tennessee." Your body and awareness are split. When you live this way you not only miss out on the present, you create tension, anxiety and dis-EASE. I call this lifestyle attitude Body Awareness Split (BAS).

GEBA Therapy is a method to help you bring your body and your awareness back together. GEBA stands for GEstalt Body-Awareness. When you have GEBA, you live your life in the present. You allow yourSELF to experience your life as it happens from moment to moment. You have your body and your awareness together. They form a whole — a Gestalt, as they say in German. Through this book you can learn HOW to have Gestalt Body-Awareness and HOW to integrate this new lifestyle attitude into everyday living. Throughout the book, "attitude" refers to the relationship of your awareness to your body.

GEBA will introduce you to a new world, a world right in your own body, a world that will take you into a space you never dreamed

1

existed, a world you can explore for a lifetime. In this space you will be able to find energy for healthful living and emotional growth. You will get in touch with your very nature, with yourSELF, by following the language of your body. You will follow your **feelings**, not your thoughts. Once you enter this space you will be able to lose your worries and your tension, gain energy you did not know you had, and with practice, completely change your attitude about your life. Through GEBA Therapy you can come to know your body, yourSELF from within. Using this method, you can learn to influence vital body functions and to change the attitudes that shape your way of life. You will become your own expert. But no matter how far you go, the results can only be greater health, more energy, less tension, and continued emotional growth.

STRUCTURE OF THE BOOK

The book is divided into five weeks. During each weekly section, you will be introduced to a new routine. Although the book presents the routines over a five-week time period, your individual progress may vary. You might progress at a faster or a slower rate or in spurts and jumps, depending on your personal nature. Time is not important. It is only important that you can successfully experience each routine before going on to the next one. You will soon know when to continue practicing a routine or when to move on to the next. The only true criterion throughout the book is your own experience.

I have written this book primarily for two people working together on different routines which I call **explorations**. The book is addressed directly to the person who will play a supportive role in these explorations. This person will read the book and relay the necessary instructions to his friend, who will actually be doing the different explorations. I use the masculine gender (he) throughout the book for the sake of simplicity only. You can adapt it to your own situation, changing it to the feminine if you work with a woman or to the plural if you work with a group. So, if you are now reading this book alone, choose a friend you are close to, someone you can rely on, to explore with you. You will read the explorations from the book and guide your friend through them. I will call you the **agent** and your partner the **friend** (or the **explorer**). At every natural break in the explorations, you and your friend will be encouraged to reverse roles. You will then become the **explorer** and your friend will become the **agent**. In this way both of you can capture the total feeling of GEBA Therapy by assuming the active role and the supportive role at different times.

In each weekly routine, GEBA Therapy presents various supportive practices, energy explorations, and sonance explorations. SUPPORTIVE PRACTICES bring you into direct body contact with

your friend. Through his touch and body manipulation, you become more aware of your body. ENERGY EXPLORATIONS help you surrender yourSELF and reach the energy state. The energy state is experienced somewhere between being awake and being asleep. You have probably been in this state before for brief periods of time without ever stopping to explore it or feel what it is like. It is a state which opens up a whole new world for you. In this state you feel calm, relaxed and recharged with energy. Your awareness centers on your body sensations and feelings rather than on your thoughts. The energy state is basic to GEBA Therapy. SONANCE EXPLORATIONS help you to integrate yourSELF. You develop a sense of the different areas in your body, become aware of their relationship to each other and to your body as a whole. This you do through breathing. Your breathing, as I will show you, is a very powerful life force in your body. Through breathing you will get in touch not only with your body but also with your deepest feelings that have been bound in your body. I call these bound feelings **energy blocks** and will talk about them later in the book. Sonance explorations help you to free energy through breathing and make it available for everyday living.

I recommend that you read through the book once to get the general feeling of how it will go, then have your friend read through the book for the same purpose. Afterwards, you both will be ready to begin.

A word of warning: You have to DO this book! The message is in **your experience**. Only by doing the explorations will you gain deeper insight into your body, into yourSELF. You cannot "head trip" the book and get it. So relax. Allow yourself an hour a day for the next several months, and then begin this journey.

If for any reason you feel strongly that you want to do this work alone, it is entirely possible to do so. Follow your feelings. Read the book carefully through first. I will act, through the book, as your agent. Since you will not have the benefit of a friend for verbal

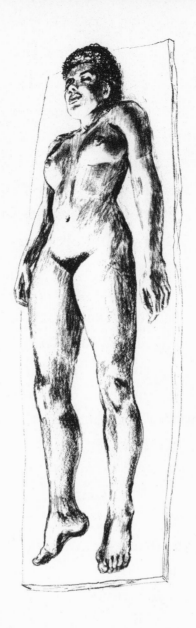

feedback, you can keep a written journal or use a tape recorder for this purpose. I will give more explicit instructions on how to do this later in the book.

The main problems you encounter working alone are lack of support, lack of feedback and the necessity to continue motivating yourself to keep going should you become impatient or afraid. Fear, brought on by your own progress, will immediately and seriously inhibit your own future advancement. As in anything else, you are your own worst enemy. Should you begin to impede your own development, I would recommend including a friend in your work.

GEBA Therapy can also be done in groups, either with one agent for the entire group or by dividing the group in half. One half of the group can be **agents** and the other half, **explorers**. I have used different combinations based on age, sex, or personal relationship, like man-woman, man-man, wife-husband, mother-daughter, friend-friend, etc.

SELECTING THE RIGHT MILIEU

Before you actually start the first exploration, I want to emphasize the importance of choosing the proper working area. Particularly in the beginning, all the elements which allow for absolute privacy are very important. So first of all, you must pick a good time of day, a time when your children are in school, when there are no direct demands on you, when you are not going to be interrupted by somebody on the phone or at the door. Also, it is not a good idea to schedule the session just before an important event, when you might not have enough time and may feel rushed in the middle of the session. The same is true about possible eating conflicts. Although it is not necessary to do this work on an empty stomach, definitely do not practice the explorations immediately following a meal. The pressure of a full stomach will keep your attention away from other sensations going on in your body. You can continue with your daily life as always, but make sure the time you choose for exploring is conducive to this kind of work.

The next question to consider is where to work. Here again, choose a place where you will have silence and privacy. The temperature in the area should be comfortable for working in the nude or lightly dressed. The lighting in the room should be rather dim. You should choose a place where you feel very much at home, where you don't anticipate any form of tension or conflict and where you feel secure. This of course, could be in your bedroom, in a park outdoors, or even at your office. Let the physical set-up help create the mood. Most of the explorations in GEBA Therapy are done in a supine position (lying on your back). The floor is an ideal work surface. You can lie down on a blanket, a foam rubber pad, a sheet, or your own carpet. The surface should not be too soft. For this reason I recommend the floor rather than a bed or couch. Whenever supportive practices are involved, you will need a hard surface to work against.

P.S.: Visit the bathroom before you start with the routines!

HOW TO DRESS

After you have chosen your time and location, consider next your choice of clothing. I recommend that you and your friend do these explorations in the nude or with very light and loose clothing. You should definitely rid yourself of any articles that cut into your skin or restrict your movement. Avoid wearing sweaters, body shirts, jump suits, belts, bras, girdles, elastic in anything, underwear or socks, tight collars, wristwatches or articles that press on the body and take your attention away from yourself. Also in this category include jewelry, sunglasses, prescription glasses and contact lenses (so you can relax your eyes completely and do not feel any pressure). I have learned through experience that if I tell people where I have placed their glasses, they can relax easier, knowing that they are in a safe place. The same is true about jewelry or valuables. Nothing should interfere with a generally relaxed climate in the room and in yourself. Another important factor is that you, as the agent, should see as much of your friend's body as possible. Only by actually seeing him can you gain an insight into your friend's feelings. This becomes particularly important when you are playing a supportive role, helping him get more in touch with himself.

THE BODY POSITION

You are the agent. Ask your friend to lie down on his back as straight and as relaxed as possible. After he has lain down, ask him to close his eyes. Now really look at your friend. Be sure that his body is straight, that his arms are by his sides, slightly turned, and that his hands are not "holding on" to the floor. Ask him to experiment with the position of his legs. Tell him to get in touch with his legs, to put his awareness into his legs and find out if he would rather have them closer together or wider apart. Be sure your friend is not touching himself or any other person or object except the floor with any part of his body. Some people prefer to have a small pillow or a folded blanket under their head. It is up to you to be supportive to your friend, to help him find the most comfortable way of lying down. At this time there is no body contact between you and your friend, but you are sitting close to him. If your friend is on a bed or couch, pull up a chair. I advise you to sit on the right side of your friend if you are right-handed and on the left side if you are left-handed. If you work on the floor, try sitting on your heels or cross-legged on a little pillow. Find a position in which you can sit comfortably for a long time. You should sit about chest high in order to get a good look at your partner's eyes, face, and torso. Once your friend is comfortable and you have each found the right position, you can start with the preliminaries. Your positions now will be your basic working arrangement throughout the book.

SUPPORTIVE PRACTICES

Supportive practices are ways you can give support and sustenance to your friend and can help him become more aware of his body and of himself. His body is an indication of the way he lives. The way he lives becomes engrained in his body in much the same way weather molds a tree. The emBODYments of tension are the direct manifestation of the type of attitude your friend holds toward his life. The attitude is like the "weather" behind his lifestyle. It embodies itself in his body as the wind determines the direction a tree will grow. When you are consistently "uptight," your body is up and tight. When you are defensive, your body moves defensively. How? By the way you walk, stand, sit, eat, make love, and breathe. The attitude behind all of these activities is emBODYed in you by the way you live. It is expressed in your body through your level of tension and your manner of carriage (your posture).

Tonicity is the natural state of balance between tension and relaxation. With this book you can learn to release and center yourself and thereby exchange your "brittleness" for resiliency. You will attain better TONICITY and CONTACT as you go along. It is common for people to use alcohol, drugs, and all kinds of gadgets and manipulations in order to rid themselves of their problems by decreasing their awareness of them. This is NOT what I mean by supportive practice. Through supportive practices you will help your friend get in touch with his problems. You will not attempt to **remove** the problems **for** him. This he will have to do himself by changing the attitude behind his problems, **his way of life**. Only then will he ever be able to live a life free from anxiety and tension. And unless he does it himself, the relief will be dependent on sources of energy outside himself and will only be temporary. He can fill himself up with pills or jump onto the massage table, but the relief is shortlived. He hasn't confronted himself. He hasn't changed his attitude.

This book will introduce you to different supportive practices. When you do them, always remember that the emphasis is never on your technique but on the attitude of your friend. Let's start with a simple supportive practice. Establish physical contact with your friend by holding his hand. The hand is the highest contact area in the human body. We touch with our hands more than with any other part of the body. Therefore, by holding your friend's hand when you talk to him about his apprehension, you are giving him security, establishing trust and telling him that you are present. You are not doing anything **for** him. He continues to have his own experience. But now he feels your presence and is not alone.

While you are holding your friend's hand, you are talking to him. Your voice in itself is a supportive practice. The way you speak sets a particular mood in the same manner a touch does. The voice you use should convey patience, comfort, and acceptance. Any pressures or excitement are not conducive to the setting. The more you put your friend at ease, the less you interfere, the more you let your friend take over, the more support you will be giving.

The moment you are in body contact with your friend, you can transmit a mood or feeling by varying the amount of pressure you apply and the way you apply it. A slow, firm contact motion communicates a sense that "all is well." Rapid or interrupted contact communicates excitement and may raise fear. Therefore, avoid quick and jerking movements and don't break contact. It is also important how much of your own hand touches your friend. Small contact areas are usually more disturbing and pain-arousing, while a touch with the entire hand has a more soothing effect.

In order to assure the right contact, I often use a lubricant. It will reduce the friction and let you adjust the amount of friction you want to have between your hand and your friend's body. (The more hair your friend has on his arms or legs, the more oil you will need.) For this purpose I use a processed olive oil (an olive oil with the smell removed). To this I add a few drops of eucalyptus oil. Together this makes an ideal mixture of an organic oil which is readily absorbed by the skin. The lubricant is very inexpensive. I use it in an eight-ounce plastic bottle with a screw cap and nozzle for easy refilling and controlled dispensing. If you fill it with only three or four ounces, it is practically spill-proof.

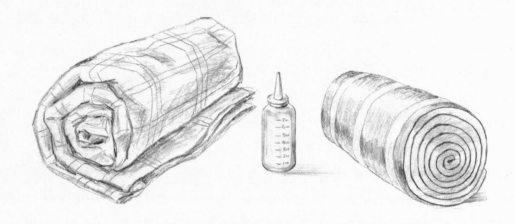

I also use a small pillow, rolled blanket or piece of foam rubber to put underneath the explorer's feet, knees, chest, or head during certain supportive practices. For this purpose you can roll up anything which will elevate and cushion the specific part of the body. I will discuss this more fully later.

VERBAL EXCHANGE

When you are taking the agent role and working with a friend, you will be asking your friend from time to time to describe to you what he is feeling. This dialogue between you both will go on prior to the routine, during the explorations, and after the whole routine is over. The verbal exchange serves several purposes. It helps you both to alleviate the first apprehension and to handle the initial fear. It is also used to communicate my instructions in the book and to answer questions. Your friend will share the sensations happening in his body with you so that you can assist him with supportive practices. Also, by verbalizing his feelings, he achieves a fuller experience of them. He is putting the language of his body into words. They are the voice of his sensations, emotions and motions. Verbalization also provides a record of his experiences and progress. It is very important for him to realize that there are no "answers" in these verbalizations. The "answers" are in his experiences, in what he sees, feels, does, or senses. After he has gone through these experiences, he will know what I mean. In GEBA Therapy you **definitely do not explain or analyze anything.**

KEEPING A RECORD

Encourage your friend to keep a journal. He should write down anything which occurs in a session, anything from "My left ear was itching" or "My left leg felt numb" to "I had the distinct feeling that I didn't have any hands" or "I got very frightened and then a great anger came up in me" and so on. Perhaps as agent you can record your friend's statements after the session. Another excellent way to keep a journal is by using a tape recorder. If you don't have access to a cassette-type recorder, perhaps some of your friends will. Not only will the journal, however you keep it, be useful to you and your friend as a guideline to your progress, it can be an exciting way to describe GEBA Therapy to someone else.

A journal will be of particular importance to you if you work alone. When you have a friend as agent, the friend provides feedback for you. When you work alone, the journal can serve as a reminder of where you have been and as a preparation for your next session. A journal is particularly helpful when working on any personal problems of living. However as in everything else in GEBA Therapy, DO NOT keep a journal if you find yourself resistant to the idea. Do not overrule you own feelings and intuition. Go with them.

ANTICIPATION AND APPREHENSION

Right now, as you get started with the preliminaries, you and your friend will probably experience some apprehension, a certain amount of distrust and fear of what could happen to you during these explorations. You anticipate the experience beforehand. You have certain expectations. You are apprehensive. This is a very natural reaction. Anticipation is just another word for anxiety and anxiety is what we feel in one degree or another whenever we approach a new experience, an unknown. We also have all been taught not to show fear, to cool it, to remain calm and try to resist our body feelings. Well, in GEBA Therapy (from the very beginning) you go "with" your body. **You put your awareness into your body.** If you feel any apprehension, it's all right to feel it. Help your friend get in touch with it by talking to him about it. For instance, you could say to him:

> How does this anticipation manifest itself
> in your body? Is your mouth dry? Do you
> feel your heart beating a little faster? Do
> you sense a tension in your throat, neck,
> or around your mouth? Perhaps your
> eyelids twitch?

All these kinds of things are natural body reactions, natural anticipatory responses. One way to start GEBA Therapy is simply to lie down, close your eyes and put your awareness into your body. Experience whatever you feel; go with your apprehension. It's all right to feel apprehensive. It always amazes me how frightened some people get by just closing their eyes and listening to themselves. These same people, however, will **unquestioningly** expose themselves to all kinds of chemical remedies like drugs, alcohol, and manipulations from rolfing to electroshock — whatever the "doctor" prescribes. They are not afraid of these things as long as they don't have to take responsibility for themselves. But the moment they are asked to respond to their body, they freak out. This might be happening to your friend now. If so, you can provide sustenance for him. Help him to get in touch with his apprehension. By doing so, he will become familiar with it, learn to accept it, and will be able to go with it rather than fight it and try to suppress it. Fighting and suppressing apprehension requires energy. And this energy will only conflict with the energy in the body trying to **express** the apprehension. When this conflict exists, we say that a person's energy becomes **blocked** or **energy ceases to be available**. And when it ceases to be available, it becomes bound in the body; it is emBODYed. We cannot really explain how this process takes place, but everybody experiences it. How? Here are some examples of emBODYed energy blocks: depression, hemorrhoids, nervous tension, indigestion, chest pains, neck and shoulder aches, stomach upset, insomnia, teeth grinding, migraine headaches, ulcers. If you and your friend recognize these or similar symptoms in yourselves, talk about them. Get in touch with them. Each is a manifestation of your body energy that is bound by conflicting forces. You are split. Part of you wants to express a feeling while part of you wants to suppress it. GEBA Therapy is a way for you to work yourself through these impasses in your life, a way toward energy, health, and emotional growth. It won't always be easy going, but it sure is worth the effort.

GROWING UP HURTS, BUT STAYING THE SAME HURTS MORE.

THE FIRST WEEK

THE FIRST WEEK

Now we are ready to begin. Your friend is lying down and you are sitting next to him as I have described in the previous pages. Let me emphasize that there is nothing that is "supposed" to happen to your friend now; **whatever** does happen is okay. Your friend is just going on an exploration. As you talk to your friend throughout this exploration, speak quietly, calmly and intimately. First of all, hold your friend's hand and establish eye contact with him. Ask him if he feels comfortable and check his body position. Ask him to move his arms, legs and body and then settle down into a comfortable position. Now tell him to **close his eyes** and keep them closed until the session ends. After he does, start a little dialogue with your friend. Ask questions like:

> What do you feel right now, this minute? Do you feel any tightness anywhere? Where do you feel apprehension? In your cheeks, around your mouth, in your chest? Are your eyes moving around in your head? Do you feel resistance to keeping your eyes closed? Keep them closed but stay in touch with your resistance.

Here you are asking your friend to get in touch with his body sensations by stating what he feels. Ask him about every part of his body that moves, twitches, or appears tense. Once he describes the sensations, ask him to focus his attention on them. Assure him that it is acceptable to feel as much or as little as he does. Even if he feels nothing, it is all right. As he continues, he will experience more and more. A slow start should not be discouraging. It is just an indication of where the person is at.

In order to prepare your friend for the first energy exploration, you must help him to become more aware of his body, hands, arms, legs, and feet. Start with his hands since you have already established direct body contact there. Tell him to put his awareness into the hand you hold. Ask him to get a visual image of it. Then touch his lower arm and ask him to get an image of that area. Touch his upper arm in

the same way. Then switch over to his other side. Begin with the hand again, then the lower arm and then the upper. Ask him to put all of his attention into the specific part that you are touching. By touching a part of his body, it becomes easier for him to put his awareness there and to form a visual image of it than if there were no contact. Now go to his feet. Hold on to his right foot with both hands and tell him to shift all of his awareness into his right foot. Now do the same thing with the lower leg and the thigh. Move over to the left foot, then the left lower leg and finally the left thigh. Gently but firmly apply as much of your hand as possible to each area you contact. Ask your friend to tell you how it feels to wander through his body from the inside as you touch it on the surface. Finish by gently pressing the stomach and chest. Finally, ask him to put his awareness into each part of his body that is in contact with the ground.

THE FIRST ENERGY EXPLORATION

In this first energy exploration, your friend will experience "heaviness" first in his limbs, then in all the rest of his body. Along with this feeling of heaviness, he will eventually drift into an awareness state which is somewhere between being awake and being asleep. I call this space the **energy state**. There is nothing to be worried about in this state. On the contrary, assure your friend that he will feel very relaxed and recharged with energy after the exploration. Ask your friend to open his eyes and look at you. Then tell him the following:

> In order to do the first energy exploration, you will close your eyes again but this time we will not be in any kind of physical contact. You will concentrate on the words I am going to say and you will repeat them to yourself. So, for instance, when I say to you "my right arm is heavy," you tell yourself, "my right arm is heavy." I will leave enough time for you to repeat exactly what I have told you before going on, but not so much time that you drift into other thoughts. Try to occupy yourself with my voice and then with your own voice. Get in touch with the desired feeling of heaviness in the respective part of your body.

Ask your friend if he understands the procedure and clear up any misunderstandings. Your friend should not repeat your directions **out loud** but only to himself. At this point it might be advisable to read the first energy exploration to him once so he gets a general idea of the sequence. Here is the **first energy exploration**:

I surrender mySELF

my right arm is heavy
my right hand is heavy
my right arm is sinking into the ground
my right arm is heavy

my left arm is heavy
my left hand is heavy
my left arm is sinking into the ground
my left arm is heavy

my right leg is heavy
my right foot is heavy
my right leg is sinking into the ground
my right leg is heavy

my left leg is heavy
my left foot is heavy
my left leg is sinking into the ground
my left leg is heavy

my arms are heavy
my legs are heavy
my arms and legs are heavy
my body is heavy

I surrender mySELF
My body is heavy

(Wait 30 seconds)

Tell him that there are different ways to get in touch with these words. He might repeat them silently to himself and put his awareness into speaking the words or into hearing them. Or he could actually have a visual image of the words as if they were on a filmstrip — MY RIGHT ARM IS HEAVY. I worked with a woman in my practice who could reproduce my voice — Viennese accent and all — in her own mind. If you do these explorations alone, you can record and play back your own voice or the voice of another person, or you can just say the words silently to yourself. If you make the recording, be sure to pause after each statement.

After you finish saying the last line of the first energy exploration — "my body is heavy" — give your friend thirty seconds to let the whole experience sink in. Then introduce him to a special sequence to terminate the energy exploration. I call it "coming out." Repeat the following words to your friend:

My face is cool
my face is nice and cool
my face is cool

make fists
open your fists
take a deep breath
stretch out

(Wait 30 seconds)

open your eyes

During the second part of the "coming out," your friend should actually make fists, take a deep breath and stretch out the way one does in the morning. This stretching in many cases initiates a yawning reflex in the person. If this happens, tell him to let the yawning take over so he can feel it in his jaws, in his tongue, in his brow, in his eyes, and try to let it move all the way into the chest and down into the diaphram and the limbs. This yawning then can become a total body experience. Finally you will ask your friend to put his arms next to himself again, wait 30 seconds, and open his eyes. He should be in the same position he assumed at the beginning of the exploration.

Let's do it. Tell your friend that you are going to break contact with him and that he should **close his eyes.** Say out loud in a calm and easy-going voice:

I surrender mySELF

my right arm is heavy
my right hand is heavy
my right arm is sinking into the ground
my right arm is heavy

If you repeat in your own mind the sentence that you have just said out loud, you will get a feeling for the amount of time that must pass in order for your friend to repeat these lines to himself.

my left arm is heavy
my left hand is heavy
my left arm is sinking into the ground
my left arm is heavy

my right leg is heavy
my right foot is heavy
my right leg is sinking into the ground
my right leg is heavy

27

my left leg is heavy
my left foot is heavy
my left leg is sinking into the ground
my left leg is heavy

my arms are heavy
my legs are heavy
my arms and legs are heavy
my body is heavy

I surrender mySELF
my body is heavy

After you finish the first exploration, wait thirty or so seconds, then start with the "coming out":

My face is cool
my face is nice and cool
my face is cool

make fists
open your fists
take a deep breath
stretch out

(wait 30 seconds)

open your eyes

Talk to your friend quietly about his experience. Heaviness can be experienced many different ways. Here is a list of possible questions to help him get started:

Was it difficult for you to keep your eyes closed? Did you actually feel any part of you getting heavier and heavier? Which part of your body seemed to get heavier the easiest? Your left arm? Your right arm? Your legs? How did you experience my voice? Could you actually see the words or could you hear my voice in your head? Did your own voice repeat my directions? How did you feel you experienced the heaviness of your body? Was it like floating down a river or was it like levitating? Were you hanging in the air or maybe floating in water? Was any part of your body lighter or heavier than another? Which part of the body? Did you have a feeling that you were actually rising out of your body? Did you feel a general relaxation all over? Did you feel the heaviness more in your actual extremities or more in your joints? Were you aware of your body moving in any way, spinning or tilting or rotating? Did you have any kind of sensations in your body? Any tingling or numbness, any vibrating or other sensations? Did you become aware of any kind of visual image? Did you see any color spots, any objects, or did you have a dream-like experience? Were your eyelids quivering? Did you get cold or warm? Were you aware of beginning to drift into the energy state which I described to you? If you did, what kind of an experience was it to you? How would you describe it? Could you concentrate easily on my words and on repeating these words? Were you aware of any kind of apprehension or fear? Were you talking to yourself about other things, so that it was difficult to concentrate on the exploration?

Perhaps this is a good time to tell your friend that if he should ever become panicky, he should feel free at any point to shift into the "coming out" by just telling himself:

My face is cool
my face is nice and cool
my face is cool

make fists
open your fists
take a deep breath
stretch out

(wait 30 seconds)

open your eyes

He can move out of the energy exploration on his own or he can tell you that he wants to come out. And then you can lead him out. This is another way you can provide sustenance and protection. It is one advantage of working with an agent in the beginning until you become comfortable working alone. The "coming out" is designed primarily for the purpose of preventing headaches created by a rapid transition into the awakened state. It also gives the explorer a feeling of security and control over himself. He will be recharged, alert and relaxed at the end. Ask your friend specifically about the "coming out":

Did you feel your face really getting cooler? Did you feel a resistance in yourself toward making fists? How did your feelings change during the "coming out"?

Many people feel this resistance and this is an excellent opportunity for you to underline the fact that they really have the power to make a fist. Your friend is in control. But he can resist himself like he can surrender himself. It is an important point to make that even if you as the agent are saying the words, **it is your friend who is in charge**. He is giving the orders to himself and he has the power to get out of any exploration whenever he wants to. Tell your friend that in the beginning it is not advisable to stay in the energy state more than thirty seconds after you say: "I surrender myself. My body is heavy."

Your first four weeks of energy exploration are a preparation for the standard energy exploration, which is basic for further work in the energy state. Once in a while people are apprehensive about allowing themselves to slide into the energy state. They get frightened and worried that they will lose control over themselves by falling into some mysterious hypnotic trance. **This will not happen**. It is important that you have the trust of your friend. This way you are helping him trust himself. Experience will teach him that he can get into the state and out of the state **at will**. He is in control of himself.

Hand this book over to your friend. Let him become an agent for you now. You lie down, relax, close your eyes and surrender **yourSELF** to the experience of your inner world.

ENERGY EXPLORATION SCHEDULE

I suggest that you practice the energy explorations twice a day. Good times to practice are shortly after waking up in the morning and in the late afternoon when you have reached a low energy point and are in need of recharging. But here again, you can experiment with different times in order to find one that is best for you. Practicing twice a day is only an arbitrary suggestion on my part. If you only have time for one session per day, do it once. If you can do it three times, do it three times. It is not important how many times you practice, but it is extremely important that the conditions during your practice time are right for GEBA Therapy.

As far as the schedule is concerned, **it is important to experience heaviness in your body first** before beginning the second energy exploration. The same is true about the other three energy explorations. Don't try to work for a calm pulse before you can get your center warm. And likewise, don't try to experience "the air is breathing me" before you can get a calm pulse. You will need to master these four separate explorations in order to combine them into what I call the standard energy exploration, which is the key to advanced exploration in the energy state. Once you can get heavy, get your center warm, have a calm pulse and the feeling that the air is breathing you, you will be able to get into the energy state relatively fast. From then on you are more or less on your own and can then try special routines. I will suggest some of them later on in the book and will show you how you can develop your own. You will learn to custom-design energy explorations that work for your specific needs, which you can do by yourself for yourself.

So, in order to learn to experience heaviness in your body you should try to practice the first energy exploration about twice a day everyday of the week. The same will be true for the second, third, and fourth energy explorations. As soon as you can achieve the desired experience with each, go on to the next one. When you can do all four energy explorations, you are ready to combine them into the standard energy exploration.

IF YOU GET SCARED

The next experience I will introduce you to is sonance exploration. When you begin sonance exploration, you breathe deeply and concentrate on the different sensations you feel in your body. If you have sensations like tingling, numbness, or cold hands, such feelings shouldn't be too threatening to you and you can experience them without too much apprehension. But sometimes in the very early stages of GEBA Therapy, breathing activates more than just mild sensations and threatening emotions begin to surface. When this happens to you for the first time you will be surprised by the spontaneous quality of the experience. If you possibly can, stay with the emotion and allow yourSELF to go with whatever you are feeling.

For instance, if the quivering of your upper lip leads to an overall feeling of sadness, **allow** yourself to be sad. **Allow** the tears to run down your cheeks. **Allow** yourself to crinkle up your face and weep. It is all right to let this happen to yourself.

The surfacing of emotions and actions and the consequent process of surrendering to them are central to GEBA Therapy.

It is possible that you might get in touch with certain feelings that are extremely threatening to you during the first sonance exploration. You might feel overpowered by your inner resistance to deep breathing. You might feel that something bad will happen or that you might be unable to stop breathing when you want to. If you can't work through these feelings and cannot handle them, switch immediately to regular breathing through your nose. If this still does not relieve your apprehension, turn over onto your front side. You will feel more protected in this position. When you look at the human body, you can imagine the back as your shell. In other words, when you are threatened, you protect your front side, which is your soft and vulnerable side. Lying face-down, you protect your vulnerable areas with the big muscle masses on your back. You don't have to face yourSELF.

If you are still scared, hold your breath at the top of an inhalation and then slowly count to six. One ... two ... three ... four ... five ... six .... Then exhale. Inhale again, hold your breath and count to six, etc. Do this four or five times and you will feel your anxiety diminish. When you are completely at ease again, start the sonance exploration routine all over again. If the anxiety returns while you are breathing deeply, try to stay with it. Keep breathing and do not terminate the exploration. If you stay with it, you will soon be able to allow yourSELF to be anxious. In this way you work through your anxiety and recognize it for what it is. This recognition will lessen your anxiety and allow for further exploration. However, if you quit the exploration all together when you become frightened, this anxiety will stay with you in the future as it has been with you until now. By staying in touch with your anxiety, it becomes more familiar to you. This is the key to eventually freeing yourSELF from its power. Now help your friend to understand that.

FIRST SONANCE EXPLORATION

Sonance comes from the Latin **sonare**, to sound. If you are sonant, you sound good. You breathe well. You give off good vibrations. You have SONANCE. While energy explorations help you to get in touch with your body energy, sonance explorations help you to integrate this energy into every part of your body. How? Through breathing. The breathing cycle is basic to GEBA Therapy. Show me how you breathe and I will tell you how you live. Through your breathing, you integrate yourSELF. When you are well-integrated, your body will hum like a smooth-running engine. After you have done sonance explorations for awhile, you will become aware of a high-frequency vibration, a kind of buzzing, in different parts of your body. Most people, when they first start their sonance explorations, are very apprehensive and have all kinds of "strange" feelings during the first stages. Where do these sensations and emotions come from? Well, the moment you breathe deeply, more energy becomes available in your body. Where there is energy flow, there is motion. You can experience this motion in many different ways: as sensations like tingling, numbness, or vibration or as emotions such as sadness, joy or anger and finally as actual body movements that go with these emotions, like crying, laughing or striking out. So, therefore, if you are afraid to feel, one of the most effective ways to keep yourself from feeling is to control your breathing.

Breathing is a natural human function. **You cannot over-breathe yourself.** You cannot hurt yourself breathing. The energy state and the breathing cycle described in this book have been used for thousands of years by people to get in touch with their bodies — with themSELVES. What is believed by some people today to be very mystical is really very pragmatic. You breathe, you touch your emotions, and you learn to know yourSELF. And breathing is where you can begin to work on yourself. By doing this part of GEBA Therapy, you can open up a new world for yourself, a world that will introduce a new attitude into your everyday life. So, if you feel some apprehension in the beginning, **go with your apprehension**. Respect it. If your body gets too defensive, don't push it. In time you will learn to trust yourself, to have patience with yourself, and to stay with the process for longer periods.

Through sonance explorations you will experience the different qualities of breathing. Breathing is not just an air exchange. It is a way of life. It is the way life is emBODYed in you. Your attitude toward your life manifests itself in the way you breathe. You know that when you are excited, your breathing becomes shallow and rapid. When you are calm, your breathing becomes slower and deeper. Your breathing takes on the quality of your life. Most people control themselves by controlling their breathing. By controlling it, they stifle their own feelings and instead of doing what they **feel** like doing, they do what they **should** do, or what somebody else tells them is the "right" thing to do. For instance, instead of conflicting with someone, they literally "hold their breath" or "swallow their feelings." Sonance explorations can help you find the way back to natural breathing and thereby to this buried part of yourSELF.

Let's do it! The preliminary conditions for sonance exploration are the same as they were for energy exploration. Have your friend lie down and sit next to him. Before he begins the actual sonance exploration, you will do a series of supportive practices together which will help your friend become more aware of his breathing. First, tell your friend to breathe through his nose and to focus his attention on his breathing. Gently place your hand on top of his hand. Explain to him that the moment he starts to think about his breathing, he will notice that he can make choices concerning it. He can stop at the end of the inhalation, or stop at the end of the exhalation. Remind him that there is no "right" way to breathe. The right way to breathe **IS** already. The right way to breathe happens when he stops interfering with his breath. It will happen eventually. **Your friend will know when he is breathing naturally.**

Now while your friend is breathing, it is important for you to observe him. Look closely. Do you detect his heartbeat in the lower part of the throat, or just underneath the rib cage? As your friend breathes, look for movement in his chest and in his lower abdomen. Many people don't move their chest or abdomen at all. If this is true of your friend, the following supportive practice will help him to increase his awareness in these areas.

Put your hand on his chest and ask him to picture himself inhaling into your hand. Let him repeat this experience several times

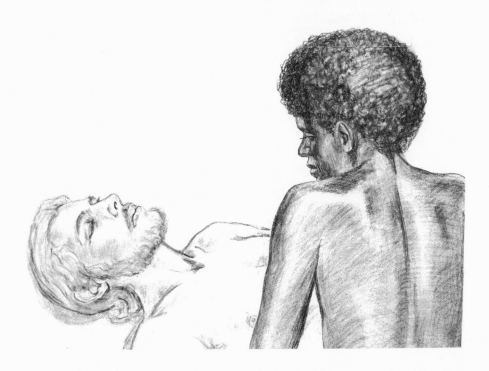

until he can put his awareness into this specific area of the body. Do the same with the abdomen. Nobody can teach him HIS way of breathing. He has to find it himself All you can do is try to help him through supportive practices to increase his awareness of his body.

As you sit next to him holding his hand, tell him that you are going to put your hand on his abdomen, just below the belly button. I call this area the **center** of the person. Now remove your hand from your friend's hand and put it on his center with your fingers spread and his belly button visible between your thumb and forefinger. You are

going to stay in contact with your friend this way throughout the sonance exploration, except during supportive practices when it is impossible for you to keep your hand on his center. Now ask your friend to **close his eyes** and to put his awareness back with his breathing. Make sure his breathing is still through his nose and is as calm and natural as possible. Tell your friend that he is going to do three sets of twenty deep breaths. Now ask him to lick his lips, open his mouth and drop his jaw. Have him shift from nose breathing to mouth breathing. Sometimes it helps to ask your friend to "inhale into your hand" which is on his center. Now you can start **the first set of twenty breathing cycles** by saying:

> Inhale into my hand ... then exhale. Inhale deeply into your abdomen and into your chest. Picture them as one big area. Now exhale through your mouth. Nice and deep. Inhale, and at the top of the inhalation, release yourself. Let go and let the exhalation take place on its own.

Ask your friend to produce a sigh of relief or of pleasure when he exhales. So it's inhale and let go ... exhale with a sigh ... Aaahhhhhhhh. At this point you might hear a restriction in your friend's throat, maybe a gargling or hissing sound that indicates that the air is not coming out easily. Remind your friend to really open his mouth, to open his throat, to let the air come in free and full. Then, at the top of the inhalation, to release himself and exhale. After about ten breaths, have your friend stop a moment and return to nose breathing. Ask him if he still feels comfortable, if he feels at all light-headed, if he feels pressure between the eyes, if his mouth is dry, or if he feels any kind of an inner resistance toward continued deep breathing. Tell him that if he does feel resistance or is aware of any of the other sensations you mentioned, that it is all right. This is what usually happens to people when they begin sonance explorations. As a matter of fact, if he would not be too threatened, he should try to get in touch with these sensations the same way he did with his apprehension at the beginning of this session. Remind him not to fight his body but to go with it! Of course, if the fear becomes overpowering he should return to nose breathing on his own. Only he can make this decision. This is true for everything he will do in GEBA Therapy from here on.

If your friend is a smoker, he might begin to cough or clear his throat. Give your friend an opportunity to take care of these reactions. Ask him if he feels comfortable enough to continue. Then you can start with another ten breathing cycles. Be sure to have your friend keep his eyes closed throughout this whole procedure. Have him begin to inhale deeply into his chest and abdomen and then release himself and exhale with a sigh. Aaaahhhhhhhhhh. And again. Inhale deeply and exhale. During this procedure your hand should remain in contact with your friend's center. If you watch your friend's face now you might begin to notice some changes: a little bit of tightness around the mouth, a twitching movement in the lower face, a nervous licking of the lips, a stretching of the throat, an uncomfortable feeling in the chest. Look at these manifestations and try to get a feeling for them. Concentrate on your friend. Try to feel what your friend feels.

When he has completed the first twenty breathing cycles, remind him to keep his eyes closed. Ask him to tell you if he is experiencing any kind of "sensations." Remember, sensations are tingling, muscle-twitches, numbness, shivering, cold hands, tightness, tenseness, vibrating, itching, or other body feelings. At this point it is very common to have a bit of light-headedness, pressure between the eyes, tingling in the fingers or the toes, and tightness or constriction around the mouth and throat. Have your friend name out loud each sensation he feels.

After he has finished describing his sensations, he can start **the second set of twenty breathing cycles.** Ask him to resume his deep mouth breathing. Encourage him to keep his mouth open, to bring in the air without restricting its passage. If he makes a hissing sound, tightens his lips, or presses the air out through a small mouth opening, make him aware of it. Tell him to listen to the sound of his breathing. At this point he might say that his fingers feel numb, his toes tingle slightly, that he feels a little pressure between the eyes (but during the breathing it disappears), that now he feels really much better than he did when he started out, or not so well, etc. This time try to avoid interrupting your friend's breathing. Let him have time to concentrate on himself. When he has finished the second set of breathing cycles, have him again share his experiences with you, as before.

Now you are ready to start **the third and final set of twenty breathing cycles.** Tell your friend to:

> Start breathing. Keep your mouth open. Wet your lips a little bit and keep your eyes closed. Really open your mouth and keep your throat as unrestricted as possible. Breathe in and out nice and full. Inhale deeply into my hand and exhale.

Encourage him to continue to breathe fully and deeply. Inhale and exhale. As your friend breathes, encourage him to keep his awareness in his body. Now you try to go with your friend. Wander with him through his body. Ask him quietly:

> Put your awareness into your feet . . . your calves . . . your thighs . . . your genital area and your lower abdomen . . . the area underneath my hand . . . your chest . . . your hands . . . now your lower arms . . . your upper arms . . . your shoulders . . . now your throat . . . the back of your head and your face.

By this time your friend will have finished the last twenty breathing cycles. Ask him to keep his eyes closed, and to explore his sensations verbally with you. Some people can detect at this point a high-frequency vibration, a kind of buzzing, underneath the tingling in their hands, around the mouth or in the thighs. If this happens to your friend, then tell him to put his awareness into these vibrations and to stay with them, to encourage them. After a while your friend will begin to realize that he can control the vibrations by either encouraging them to grow or by shutting them off. This knowledge will make it much easier for your friend to go with the vibrations. So, if he has vibrations in his mouth, let the vibrations really take over. Have him keep his mouth relaxed and open and give in to the vibration. As he lies silently beside you, ask him where he feels any vibrations now. If he feels them in the cheeks, then he should let the vibrations really take over in his cheeks. Perhaps his eyes will start to twitch a little. Encourage him to give in to the twitching. Really let his eyes twitch; let them move. It's all right. Have your friend continue breathing nice and easy through his nose. Just sit with him and encourage him to tell you about any sensations that are going on inside his body. When he seems to have told you everything he can, and after he can no longer detect any sensations, tell him to slowly open his eyes. At this time you can remove your hand from his center and hold his hand again while he comes out. This will finish off the first sonance exploration.

A series of three times twenty breathing cycles usually is a very good start. But always use your own intuition, and interrupt the session whenever you feel that your friend is becoming too anxious to respond openly. On the other hand, if everything goes well, your friend might even like to add a few more breathing cycles. The decision, however, really must come from him. If he feels good with the breathing and wants to go on, let him take a few more breaths. Whenever he feels very uncomfortable or very anxious, terminate the session immediately. "Don't push" is the best advise I can give. GEBA Therapy is a very gentle method. **The power lies within the process of the exploration.** There are absolutely no manipulative or aggressive techniques to apply, as there are in most psychotherapeutic systems. You as the agent are only present to support your friend and to provide him with feedback when he needs it.

After going with your friend through the first energy exploration and the first sonance exploration, you will begin to have a feeling for this method. GEBA Therapy is a spontaneous process. Every sensation, every emotion and every movement has to ripen, to come out spontaneously. The person who explores knows and feels when a situation is ripe. He will start to let himself go. Then things happen. The longer you do this work, either alone or with a friend, the more confident you will become and the more you will rely on your natural intuition and wisdom. The moment you push, the body turns against you. Instead, you must flow with it. This is why I like the method so much. It is as gentle and powerful as a flowing stream once you become a part of it. Sitting next to your friend, you can participate in his unfolding. You will see him slowly let go, slowly feel new energy, slowly relax and open up to his own deep feelings. You will encourage him to follow these feelings. And you will watch him over a period of time lose his rigidity and become supple, relax and open up to a new, stronger sense of himSELF. In the beginning, your friend will deal with sensations in different parts of his body. He will move around in his body. Later, deeper feelings will emerge. But throughout this whole process, the information (sensations, emotions, and motions) and their controls are within the explorer. As agent, you will help your friend know and feel this.

Now is a good time for you to hand this book to your friend. Let him become your agent, and you get into the first sonance exploration for yourself. After you have worked with this method awhile, your new awareness of yourself will be helpful to both of you in future explorations.

SONANCE EXPLORATION SCHEDULE

There is no "one right way" to do sonance explorations. Nobody can teach you correct breathing or tell you when to stop. Only through your own experience will you gain deeper insight into yourSELF as you go along. Keep listening to yourself. You are closer to the process than anyone else. You ARE the process.

In order to get you started with sonance exploration, I will give you an arbitrary schedule as a guideline. Everything in it is subject to your own discretion. If the schedule feels right, adopt it. If you feel like changing it, then change it! Remember, the answers are not in the schedule, in the supportive practice or in another person, but in yourSELF. Use the schedules as an aid to help you to take the first steps. The moment you begin to feel confident enough, choose for yourself which way you want to progress.

I suggest that you do the first sonance exploration once every second day. Or, in other words, go through three routines during the first week. If this arbitrary schedule feels comfortable to you, continue the same sequence for the second, third, and fourth sonance explorations.

As far as the duration of each individual routine is concerned, try three times twenty breathing cycles for the first sonance exploration, two times forty breathing cycles for the second sonance exploration, two times fifty breathing cycles for the third sonance exploration and one hundred breathing cycles for the fourth sonance exploration.

A breathing cycle starts at the moment of inhalation and is finished after the pause at the end of the exhalation. You inhale and then there is a short pause. You exhale and then there is another short pause, and at the end of this pause, the breathing cycle ends and the next cycle starts. Breathing cycles can serve as a measure for you. When you introduce your friend to sonance explorations, you give him this count as something to go by. First there are more frequent but shorter periods of breathing to give you time to verbalize and to assist your friend in dealing with his initial apprehension. Later there is only one uninterrupted block of breathing. Another way to measure the amount of breathing is with a clock. The average ratio is six to eight breathing cycles per minute. So, when you do twenty breathing cycles, you can figure it will take you about three minutes. Again, let me repeat, the recording of the time or the number of breathing cycles is **not the important thing**. The important thing is for your friend to listen to himself. These schedules only serve as an arbitrary means to give you something to go by and to get started. It won't take your friend very long to **know** when he wants to stop or when he feels like continuing his breathing. Soon he will be in touch with himself enough to design his own program entirely on the basis of his own experience and needs.

... separated are pleasure from work, the means from the end, effect from satisfaction. Eternally confined to small fragments of the whole, man himself turns into a fragment. Tuned into the monotonous grind of the wheel he never develops the harmony of himSELF and instead of integrating the humanity of his very nature he becomes a mere reflection of his business, his science. ... the dead word replaces the wisdom of living and a trained mind overpowers intuition and sensitivity.

Friedrich von Schiller (1759-1805)
translation by author

THE SECOND WEEK

IF YOU CAN'T SLEEP AND HAVE NO ENERGY

Let me start your second week's work by showing you the beginning of a typical first session in my private practice:

John: On the way over here to your office I had figured out what I was going to tell you. Now I am here and I don't know what to say. This happens to me all the time. I'm always carrying on a conversation in my mind; I can't stop thinking. I get tense. I have no energy. I am so tired at night that I can't stay up, but when I go to bed, I can't sleep. Things keep going around and around in my head. It's driving me crazy. I feel like I'm running around like a chicken with its head cut off and accomplishing very little.

Bruno: What are you thinking about?

John: Well, it's always basically the same. Why I do this or why I do that. What I'm going to do or what I should do. What I could have done or what I should have done. It's a vicious circle. And all in all, I **do** practically nothing.

Bruno: How do you feel right now?

John: I am bothered because I still haven't said what I wanted to and I don't think I've told you what you really wanted to hear.

Bruno: What I want to hear is how you feel right now.

John: Gee, I'm sorry. I'm really messed up, aren't I? How do I feel? I guess a little embarrassed and anxious.

Bruno: Close your eyes. Describe to me how you feel this anxiety. What are the actual sensations in your body that express your apprehension.

John: Well, whenever I am tense I know I start swallowing a lot. Do I have to keep my eyes closed? That's really hard for me to do!

Bruno: Yes, if it isn't too threatening for you, keep your eyes closed and tune in to your body. This is where you will find the answers you are looking for.

John: When I swallow, my mouth feels dry and my neck is really tense.

Bruno: Yes, go on.

John: My hands are cold and I have a funny feeling in my stomach. I am aware of my heart beating in my chest and in my throat.

Bruno: And in your eyes?

John: Yeah, my eyelids are twitching. I can't seem to stop them.

Bruno: Why try to? Allow your eyelids to twitch.

And so forth.

This person's experiences are typical. Do you have anything in common with him? Do you feel that you are sometimes running around like a "chicken with its head cut off?" To be more accurate, you are really not the chicken at all. You are the **head**. Your wheels keep spinning and all your energy is spent. As long as you keep busy, you can distract yourself from yourSELF. You make lists of things to do, but never manage to do them. You look out the window, you go to the cookie jar, you masturbate, you telephone your friend — anything except tackle the list. Your energy is spent thinking and avoiding and there is none left for **doing**. You only **think** about doing. But even when you are busy, the work is in your head. The body never gets a chance to be active. When you come home in the evening, it's little wonder you can't turn your head off. And you aren't physically tired enough to sleep. This combination of "thinking" with no physical activity and sleep with no recharge of energy is deadly. The tension mounts in you. The engine is reving but going nowhere.

How different it is with children. They play hard and they keep their awareness in the moment. Once something is done, it is over. They don't hang on to anything or project into tomorrow. They play hard and then they sleep hard.

It is the child-like lifestyle attitude you need to rediscover for yourSELF. How can you do this? Start out by listening to your body the way John did in my office. Put this book down. Allow yourself to become fully aware of what you are feeling right now. How are you sitting or lying down? Are you comfortable or tense? What do you feel right this minute? Can you locate this feeling in a part of your body? This present sense of yourself is the only place you can be in right now. It's all right. Start from here. Practice the explorations presented in this book regularly. They will help you rediscover the attitude you lived in your childhood. The road is not an easy one and will take time. If you look for a fast solution, this isn't it! You haven't reached your present condition overnight. It will take effort and patience on your part to get back to a more spontaneous, energized lifestyle.

Here's what to do: resist pills, drugs and all other stimulants; they only dull and distort your senses. Give your body a chance to tell you how it suffers. Try to hear your body and act on what it says. If you feel "jumpy," take a walk, jog, go for a swim, etc. If you feel irritable, for instance, go into a private room, close the door and get really irritable. Express your anger. Shout who you're angry at. Lie down and kick the bed. If you can't, repeat "I am angry" over and over out loud — or just growl awhile. Make animal noises.

Continue to practice your explorations on schedule. Gradually you will learn to read your body's messages promptly and accurately, you will sleep better and feel re-energized.

YOU ARE IT

You are your own expert. When you do these energy or sonance explorations, the emphasis is on you and not on the different aspects of this method, its supportive practices, or your agent. **You are it.** Only you can put your awareness into your body, into yourSELF. The emphasis is definitely not on the amount of breathing you do but on what goes on **in you** while you breathe. Or, in other words, you will experience your progress not by the breathing you do but through the quality of contact you can establish with yourself while breathing. And by doing this, you are taking the responsibility for your own personal growth. Responsibility is the ability to respond. And to whom should you respond? To yourSELF, of course. This is the major difference between my method and other systems. The emphasis here is not on the technique, the expert therapist, or the activity itself; it is on the attitude behind whatever you are doing. You explore, you experience, you know, you change, and you grow. You are it.

When you are the agent, when you hold the book, conduct certain supportive practices, make suggestions to your friend, and observe him, remember that you are a catalyst only. Give your friend a chance to take care of his own reactions, to express them, and to deal with them in his own way. In some instances, you might even become a part of his way. That's all right. As long as it is **his** way. Your deep-rooted need to control and manipulate is based on an attitude which is diametrically opposed to the one you need to be a good agent. Your friend does the leading; you follow and support. This approach is basic to your work. Try to relax into it.

You may find it hard to sit beside your friend and do nothing while he explores. Don't do nothing. Sit in a comfortable position. Center your attention on your friend. Try to go with him in his explorations and wanderings. Follow him intuitively. **He is it.**

THE SECOND ENERGY EXPLORATION

When you and your friend have worked with the first energy exploration until he can easily get a feeling of heaviness in his body and limbs, you are ready to start with the second energy exploration. This new energy exploration calls for the same conditions and preparations as before. The only thing that changes is your friend's focus. Instead of concentrating on a routine which makes him feel heavy, he will concentrate on one which will make him feel warmth in different parts of his body and in his center.

As your friend begins this second energy exploration he will say "my body is heavy." If he finds he cannot get his entire body heavy when he says this, he should go back and work further on the first exploration. The same will be true for you when your turn comes.

Energy explorations build in sequence for you. It is important to create a cumulative effect as you go, so that by the fourth week you can easily enter the energy state as I describe it. Each new exploration begins with a sentence summing up your previous week's work. As your friend goes over this part, he should experience heaviness fully, before he begins the warmth exploration.

I surrender mySELF
my body is heavy

my right arm is warm
my right hand is warm
my right arm is nice and warm
my right arm is warm

my left arm is warm
my left hand is warm
my left arm is nice and warm
my left arm is warm

my right leg is warm

my right foot is warm

my right leg is nice and warm

my right leg is warm

my left leg is warm

my left foot is warm

my left leg is nice and warm

my left leg is warm

my arms are warm

my legs are warm

my center is nice and warm

my center is warm

I surrender mySELF

my center is warm

(wait 30 seconds)

The "coming out" routine is the same as before:

my face is cool

my face is nice and cool

my face is cool

make fists

open your fists

take a deep breath

stretch out

(wait 30 seconds)

open your eyes

Before your friend starts with the actual exploration, you and your friend should try another supportive practice. Ask him to **close his**

eyes. Put your hand right on his center about one inch below his navel. Tell your friend to put all his awareness into the area of his body where he can feel your hand. Ask him to get in touch with all the feelings he has in the area underneath your hand. If you are sitting on the left side of your friend, it is better to use your left hand so that you will have his navel between the V of your thumb and forefinger.

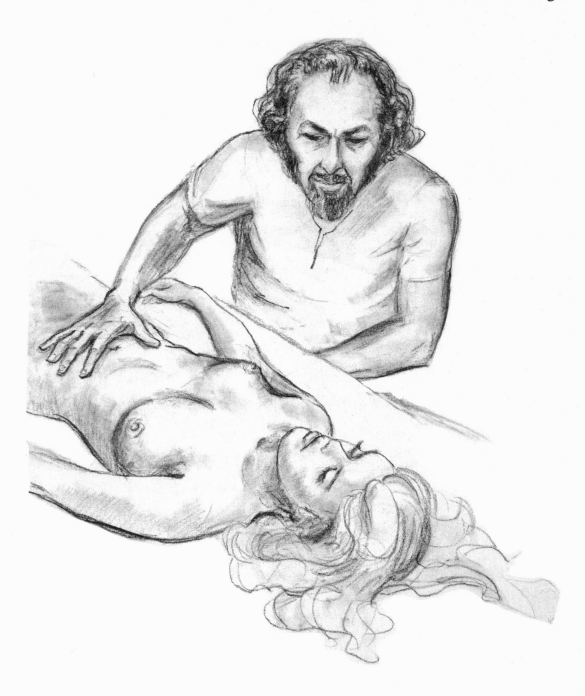

This way you can really get a complete hold on his lower abdomen. You needn't keep your hand stiff. Just let your hand be flexible as if you were really trying to cover as much of his lower abdomen as you possibly can. Remind your friend to keep his eyes closed and ask him to stay in touch with your hand. Try to tune in to the rhythm of his breathing cycle and allow your hand to move up and down with the motion of his abdomen. Tell your friend now that his center is the area he will try to make warm during this energy exploration. Because of the natural warmth of your friend's abdomen combined with the touch of your own hand, his center will feel warmer to him at this point. Ask your friend if he can feel this warmth, the warmth of your hand on his center. If he can feel it, he has a valuable experience which he can use as a reference point for the last part of the second energy exploration when he will actually **make** his center warm.

The wording of this routine does not always work for every person who tries it. Some people have to imagine the opposite condition; in order for them to get their center warm, they must imagine an ice pack on their abdomen or their feet in a bucket of ice cold water. Your friend will have to experiment for himself. This is another way **exploration** comes in.

After you have finished with this supportive practice, when your friend is sure he feels your hand's warmth, say to him:

> Now I am going to remove my hand. Close your eyes and relax as much as possible while we begin the second energy exploration. We will finish it with the "coming out" routine and then talk about your experiences afterward as we did before.

Remove your hand. Double-check your friend's body position. Now introduce the new routine:

I surrender mySELF
my body is heavy

my right arm is warm
my right hand is warm
my right arm is nice and warm
my right arm is warm

my left arm is warm
my left hand is warm
my left arm is nice and warm
my left arm is warm

my right leg is warm
my right foot is warm
my right leg is nice and warm
my right leg is warm

my arms are warm
my legs are warm
my center is nice and warm
my center is warm

I surrender mySELF
my center is warm.

(Wait 30 seconds)

my face is cool
my face is nice and cool
my face is cool

make fists
open your fists
take a deep breath
stretch out

(Wait 30 seconds)

open your eyes

Now it is time again for your verbal exchange. Ask your friend if he could experience his warmth at all. If so, where did he have the most pronounced sensation? In his arms, in his legs, in his hands or feet, on the left side of his body or on the right side of his body? Could he get his center warm? What made this experience different from the heaviness routine? Did he have any kinds of other sensations like vibrating, numbness, or pulsation? Did anything extraordinary happen? At this point you can also ask if he was aware of any visual images. Did he see anything going on behind his closed eyes? Were they in black and white or in color? What did he see? By now your friend is used to this verbalization and probably will not have any problems describing his experiences to you in his own way.

Now you can either change places with your friend and let him be your agent while you explore or you can do the second energy exploration alone. This way you can find out if you would rather work with an agent or if you would rather work alone. There is no right or wrong way to do it. You must experience which method works better for you. And it doesn't necessarily mean that you are "stronger" if you do not choose an agent. It is merely a personal preference. Sometimes circumstances will make the decision for you. You might only be able to meet with your friend a couple of times during the week. If your friend is not always available, you have to do some of your explorations alone. In this case, you either repeat the routine to yourself, use a tape recorder with your own voice or your friend's voice on the tape, visualize your words, or choose any other method that works for you. Just remember that when you practice alone you must go through the same preliminary procedures. Leave your hands at your sides but don't hold onto the ground. Be sure that your hands do not touch your own body. Then just go ahead and work in whatever way feels most comfortable to you. A good time to practice these energy explorations is immediately after you wake up in the morning and shortly before you go to bed at night. I know quite a few people who prefer to do their explorations around four or five o'clock in the afternoon just when they seem to experience a "low" in their energy level. After drifting into the energy state, they feel more relaxed, recharged and ready to finish the day with more energy available.

SENSATIONS, EMOTIONS, AND MOTION

Life is a process. A process is on-going. It moves. When you are alive, you are in motion. When you are in motion, you feel and you act. What you feel you call sensations and emotions. Here are some examples. Sensations are: feelings of numbness, cold, heaviness, itchiness, light-headedness, tension, warmth, etc. Emotions are when you feel lonely, depressed, sad, confused, restless, frustrated, happy, resentful, worried, frightened, guilty, etc. When you express these feelings through motions, you actually **move** with your feelings. You're hitting, kicking, shivering, reaching, holding, stretching, laughing, sulking, etc. Sensations and emotions are going on inside of you and motions are usually the respective outward expression of what moves you inside. Actually, they all are ways the body uses to express itself. Your cold hands (sensation) are as real as your feeling of apprehension (emotion) and the defensive action of your body (motion). An example of this would be: the blood is rushing into your genitals (sensation), you feel sexy (emotion), and you make love (motion). Sensations and feelings, therefore, can be treated as concretely as overt acts. If you were transparent, for instance, you could see yourself getting anxious, angry or uptight. You could see your blood rushing into one area and withdrawing from another. You could observe a change in the output of your heart, a spasm in your stomach wall, a tingling in your feet, etc. Sensations are not the causes of feelings; they **are** the feelings you recognize as sadness, guilt or joy. These feelings are developed in you in the same way that you learn to walk or ride a bike. They are part of how you ARE in this world.

Sensations, emotions and motions go together as a total body expression. You can express your feelings through motions or you can refuse to act and thereby block your emotions. What you can't do is interfere with the inner actions of your body once your body reacts to a situation. All you can do is to keep yourSELF from getting in touch with your feelings and thereby keep yourself from acting. The reaction of your body to a threatening situation is initiated by an automatic system which has been built into your body as a defense mechanism against danger. As long as there is real danger, this system works well. If you are scared, your body mobilizes instant energy and you utilize this energy immediately by running away. But here is the problem. You don't really have to be in a true danger situation to get your body mobilized. You can **think** one up. You can do this by anticipating what should go on tomorrow or reworking what could have happened yesterday. The big problem is that you can't act on these things right now because either they happened yesterday or they have not yet happened (tomorrow). But your body doesn't know this; it gets fooled by your head. You can remain "keyed up" and mobilized for danger for a long period of time. As long as you're in this condition, your anticipatory "thinking" keeps your body stirred up. Believe it or not, some people spend a whole lifetime in this state.

In order to escape your head, you have to bring yourSELF down into your body. You do this in GEBA Therapy by becoming aware of what is going on in your body. Through breathing, you intensify the process. You start by concentrating on your sensations. They are the least threatening body motions and therefore are relatively easy for you to experience. By following these sensations, you begin to get in touch with very subtle feelings underneath them which eventually develop into specific emotions. Along with these emotions comes the desire to express them. Once you have gone this far you will know how to make these expressions.

Let me give you two practical examples:

Sensation: throat tense, mouth dry, jaw rigid
Emotions: resentful, angry
Motion: hands form fists, strike the bed, you shout, "NO!"

Sensations: lower lip quivering, eyes full, a pressure on your chest
Emotions: depressed, sad
Motion: crying, sobbing, whispering, "It's all over."

Sonance explorations help you to discover your feelings, express them and therefore communicate clearly with yourSELF. You integrate yourSELF by freeing blocked motions. You open up blocked areas of your body by letting them carry out sensation-emotion-motion sequences. By removing energy blocks, you finish your body's unfinished business.

THE SECOND SONANCE EXPLORATION

Before you begin the second sonance exploration, I want to introduce you to a supportive practice which you will use during this session. After your friend has lain down, ask him to **close his eyes**. Squirt a little bit of oil into the palms of your hand. Then take his hand and start rubbing the oil into it with both of your hands. With

this preliminary hand contact, you are setting a certain mood depending on how you work with your friend's hand. Hold it gently but with sureness and strength. Continue rubbing the oil into his hand with both of your hands — slowly and with feeling. The kind of mood you want to create is gentle, but powerful. Your friend will experience strength and sensitivity through your touch. Now hold your friend's hand with both of your hands so that the two thumbs are on the back of his hand. His fingertips should be pointing toward you. Be sure that he does not hold his hands and arms stiff, but relaxes them in your care. You can feel the difference, whether he is "controlling" his arm or is handing it over to you. Start to apply pressure with your left thumb and your right thumb, moving in a circular motion. Push toward his

wrist with your left thumb, then right thumb, left thumb, right thumb, etc. Your grip can be pretty strong. It is a good feeling to your friend; he will sense your assurance. You should have a feeling similar to that of kneading dough.

After about fifteen strokes, you can start to work on each finger, stroking them with your thumbs on top and your forefinger underneath; go toward his palm. The pressure that you apply always moves in the direction of the heart. Stay in touch contact with your

friend. Never interrupt the contact. Check from time to time to see that your friend remains relaxed in his arms and hands and that he is not tensing them. Now you can start this same practice with his other hand. Put his hand down slowly. Don't just drop it! Put it down gently. Everything you do during the explorations should be with a deliberate but gentle action. Avoid surprises. When you start with his other hand you might have to change sides. Usually it is not necessary since you can handle his other hand by reaching over his chest. Experiment for yourself and discover where you feel most comfortable.

Now start working on your friend's other hand. First, rub the oil in using a rotary motion between your thumb and forefinger; then stroke each finger separately. When you are through with the hand, put it down carefully. Don't drop it. Now you are going to do this same practice on your friend's feet. I recommend you put a pillow or blanket, as I described in the introduction, underneath your friend's knees so that they are slightly elevated. This support should be large enough to elevate the knees about six inches. The leg can relax better if it is not over-extended.

Now start again the same way that you did with his hands. Start rubbing oil into your friend's foot. By now you already have some

experience of how you can adjust the degree of lubrication with the amount of oil you apply. If you have too much friction, then apply more oil. If your hand slides too fast and you cannot hold onto him, then wipe some oil off. Continue to be aware of the amount of pressure you apply, what speed you choose, and how much actual contact you maintain with your friend's foot. You want to give him reassurance and create a supportive milieu. Hold his foot with both of your hands with your thumb on top, as you did with the hands. Start with a circular motion on the top of the foot, once with your left thumb and once with your right thumb. After about fifteen strokes,

support the foot with one hand underneath the heel and then stroke the upper part of the foot with the other hand.

After a while you will learn to put your personal note into these practices. Just be sure that whenever you apply pressure, you apply it in the direction of the heart. Do not interrupt your motion, but continue to stay in touch with his foot. Slide back to your starting position without pressure and again press toward the heart. Many people who go through the first and second sonance explorations have their first sensations in their hands and feet. These extremities feel numb, cold, tight, or the person experiences a tingling sensation. If this is the case with your friend, work on his hands and feet. Of course, different people will have different body responses. The order I am giving you here is arbitrary. After you have gone through several weeks of this work, you will become aware of these things yourself and then you can apply whatever supportive practice seems appropriate to the situation. In my practice, I can tell by a person's reactions how far they want to go.

Listen to your friend and observe him. You will develop an intuitive feeling for sensing your friend's reaction the moment he himself experiences it. Through verbal exchange with your friend, by working with other people and above all, by doing GEBA Therapy yourself, you will continue to improve your awareness of how the body communicates.

So why don't you change places with your friend and let him give you a chance to experience these supportive practices on your hands and feet? Lie down, **close your eyes**, and try to help your friend find the pressure, speed, and type of motion that feels best to you. Describe to him the quality of some of his motions; if they are too jerky, if they are too light, or whatever reaction they bring out in you. Tell him what feels particularly good to you and remind him that he should not break contact. Surrender yourself fully to this experience. Keep as much of your awareness as you can in whatever part of you is being worked on. Take it all in!

Last week's sonance exploration consisted of three times twenty full breathing cycles. As you will remember, a breathing cycle begins with the moment of inhalation and ends after the pause following the exhalation just before you are ready to inhale again. The average full breathing rate during sonance exploration is about six or eight breathing cycles per minute. For this second sonance exploration, you will do twenty more breathing cycles than you did in the first. Instead of breaking them up into three sections of twenty cycles each week, you will have only two sequences of forty full breathing cycles each.

Get ready to start. Ask your friend to lie down, **to close his eyes**, and then put your hand on his center. Let him find his breathing rhythm by breathing through his nose only. Try to pick up his rhythm and tune in on it, letting your hand move up and down on his center. After you have looked your friend over and are sure that his position is good, ask him to wet his lips, to open his mouth and to start to breathe fully. Get him started by saying:

Inhale deeply. Release yourself. Now exhale. Inhale
deeply again. Release yourself. And exhale.

Observe your friend and listen to his breathing. Stay in contact with his breathing rhythm, the movement of his abdomen and chest, and continue to observe his body. You can learn a lot by observing your friend's body. You get a feeling for the place he is in this way. Keep an approximate count of his breathing cycles. After about twenty cycles, ask your friend if he is feeling all right and if he wants to continue. Encourage him to stay in touch with himself and to keep his awareness in his body. After about thirty full breathing cycles, remind your friend to search his body for feelings underneath his sensations. Ask him to wander through his body by putting his awareness into different areas wherever he feels tingling, numbness, vibration, etc. Ask him:

Are you aware of any special feelings? Do you feel
tears coming into your eyes? Do you feel sad? Are
you aware of any resentment? Do you feel like
laughing? Take three more deep breaths. Inhale
deeply, release yourself, and exhale. Inhale deeply
and exhale.

After forty full breathing cycles, tell him to slow down, to breathe through his nose and to remain in touch with his body. Now give him a chance to tell you about his experiences during this first part of the exploration. Sometimes the information comes out very easily. Other times, you'll have to keep asking:

Do you feel tight anywhere? Do you feel frightened?
Do you feel any tingling anywhere? Were you aware
of any emotions?

If your friend does not feel like talking or has nothing further to report ask him to resume his breathing. Tell him to:

Drop your jaw and start to breathe again — deeply
and fully. Inhale and exhale into your chest and into
your abdominal cavity. When you are on top of the
inhalation, release yourself. Just let go. Don't press
the air out. Let the exhalation happen. Give a sign
of relief or of pleasure — AAAaaahhhhhhhhh.
Inhale through your mouth and exhale.

You should continue to listen to his inhalation and exhalation. See if they take place without any resistance. If you can hear a gargling or hissing sound, tell your friend about this. Tell him to open his throat and let the air come in and out freely. Make sure that his mouth stays open. By now your friend has probably found his natural rhythm. You will recognize this rhythm when you see it. It is a wave-like motion going through his chest and abdomen together. You will also recognize a change in this rhythm when he starts to feel uncomfortable and wants to quit. If your friend reports that his fingers are tingling or his hands feel very stiff you can introduce the supportive practice you have just learned. Take his hands and work with them as you did at the beginning of this session. The same, of course, is true for his feet. If your friend reports any kind of tightness, numbness, or spastic feeling, or extreme tingling in the feet, work on them. Throughout the supportive practices, continue to observe him. After his final deep breaths completing the second set of forty cycles, tell him to switch again to regular nose breathing, to stay in contact with his body and to report to you the sensations and feelings he experiences or has experienced during the routine.

As I have pointed out before, reactions to both energy and sonance explorations vary widely with different individuals. I cannot go into all the possibilities at once and therefore I am presenting for you an arbitrarily chosen order. Generally at this point, most people experience tightness around their mouth, pressure between the eyes,

tenseness in the throat, in the legs, or in the stomach. During the second part of the second sonance exploration, they often work through this tightness and resistance to breathing, as well as their general discomfort. This leads to a freer breathing rhythm, which brings out new sensations. Underneath the tingling, most people start to get in touch with a high-frequency vibration. Some people have described it to me as a "buzzing". This is the kind of sensation that you should encourage, by saying:

Get in touch with any vibration you feel. Go with it. Let the vibration spread. Experiment with it and experience how you can get in touch with it, how you can go with it, and how you can turn it off. Go with it as much as possible. Let it spread into different areas in the body.

When a person is sonant, he is able to experience this high-frequency vibration in his whole body, from his toes to his head. And after some time, with practice, he will be able to move the vibrations into different parts of his body. So at this stage, your friend is beginning to discover the vibrations in limited areas of his body and is starting to learn how to work with them.

Another sensation your friend might experience here is visual images. He may start to see, for instance, white spots with black dots which change later into blue and green tones, and then perhaps to red, or anything else. Some people can immediately see certain objects or have dream-like experiences. As with any other experiences, encourage your friend to explore them:

Just watch. Let it be. See what happens. Go with the sensations, the visual ones, the kinesthetic ones, the sensory ones, whatever it is. It's all right.

When you are finished talking these things over with your friend, withdraw your hand from his center and ask him to open his eyes.

Change positions, so you can experience the second sonance exploration. Have a nice trip!

BREATHING IS THE GATE

What works for motion, works for emotion. There is really no difference between them. Both are body expressions. In a coordination block, you block your motion and in a feeling block you block your emotion. When emotions are blocked in your body, its normal energy flow is interrupted. When motions are blocked in your body, its normal energy flow is interrupted. Feeling blocks and coordination blocks are energy blocks. In most cases, they are closely interrelated.

Let me show you how an energy block works by using motion (movement) as an example: Skiing is the kind of sport which relies heavily on how you are standing on your skis, or in other words, on the kind of contact you have with the ground. It is typical for the beginning skier not to bend his knees and ankles. When you bend your knees and ankles, you get your flexor muscles ready to take off or to come down at any time. You are in touch with the ground and can absorb irregularities as you move over the ground. Your legs are constantly readjusting the rest of your body to the forces of gravity and motion. If you lean too far back on the skis — WHISH — the skis will slide out in front of you; if you are too far forward, you will make a header. In order to establish and maintain this delicate balance, your body and your awareness must be together. Only then are you in contact with the ground; only then will you have the right amount of tonicity (a proper balance between tension and relaxation) and contact (posture) on your skis.

Sue is a beginning skier. She does not bend her knees. Her legs are very stiff. She is on a head trip, fantasizing herself as a champion on the cover of the latest ski magazine. Also, she is just plain scared of falling. Yes, that's it. She's **scared stiff!** One thing is certain — she is not in touch with her legs. In fact, she doesn't even know she has legs. When her ski instructor yells, "Bend ze knees!" the poor girl goes through every kind of contortion except knee-bending. She hashes out her predicament with other people in the group, as if they could help her ski. She tries to figure the whole thing out in her head; she uses so much energy it just splashes all over the place. But none of it is going to her knees. They are blocked and the energy that is needed to bend them is used to keep them stiff or is wasted on other unrelated movements and on her "thinking."

The same thing happens with one's emotions. Let's take resentment. If you block this emotion, your resentment always shows up somewhere else in your body. Perhaps your jaw becomes tight and you grind your teeth. In such a case, you are as far removed from your tight jaw and your emBODYed resentment as Sue was removed from her legs and their blocked coordination. How could you help her to get in touch with her legs? In skiing, this is relatively simple. Just put one ski pole into the ground and another beside it and then a third horizontally through the leather straps so that they form a little gate. Now instead of shouting, "Bend your knees," you ask her to ski through this gate at the bottom of the hill. At first, this is easier said than done. When she tries to ski down the hill through the gate — WHAM!! She hits her head on the cross-bar. Then she goes back up the

hill asking everybody what to do — wanting explanations and expecting to figure it all out in her head. Again she comes down the hill and WHAM!! She hits her head again on the crossbar. After the fourth time, she suddenly **sees** the cross-bar for the first time. Her awareness is brought into her body. She is no longer out there with her fantasies or fears about skiing. Her awareness is finally united with her body. When she comes to the cross-bar, she just ducks. She avoids hitting her head and thereby bends her knees. Suddenly she is in touch with the ground. She is in the here and now. She has Gestalt Body-Awareness.

What works for motion works for emotion. In GEBA Therapy you use breathing the same way the ski instructor used the gate. Breathing is the gate. You probably have the same reactions toward this work that Sue had about going through the gate. You probably wonder, what does breathing have to do with my emotional growth, my well-being? "I feel so nervous. My heart is palpitating. My palms are sweating. My mouth is dry and Bruno has me lie down and breathe while he asks me how I feel in my toes, my fingers and if my lips are vibrating. What does this have to do with my emotional problem?" Through breathing, you get in touch with your body and by getting in touch with your body, you free its energy, thereby ridding yourself of tension. Through breathing, you get in touch with your body the same way the cross-bar helped Sue to get in touch with her legs. A motion, the bending of the knees and ankles, emerges from you as spontaneously as an emotion, like frustration. Once emotions are expressed, it doesn't matter any more if you explain them to anybody or not — just as it would have been anticlimatic for the ski instructor to analyze why Sue was bending her knees after she got through the gate. The answer lies in the experience, and explanations become superfluous. Breathing is the gate. It is one good way to get in touch with yourSELF.

I think I could turn and live with animals, they are so placid
        and self-contained;
I stand and look at them long and long.
They do not sweat and whine about their condition;
They do not lie awake in the dark and weep for their sins;
They do not make me sick discussing their duty to God;
Not one is dissatisfied — not one is demented with the mania of
        owning things;
Not one kneels to another, nor to his kind that lived thousands
        of years ago;
Not one is respectible or unhappy over the whole earth.
So they show their relations to me and I accept them;
They bring me tokens of myself;
They invince them plainly in their possession;
I wonder where they got those tokens;
Did I pass that way huge times ago and negligently drop them?

Walt Whitman

THE THIRD WEEK

THE ENERGY BLOCK

Remember what happened to Sue, the beginning skier? She had a coordination block. The harder she kept thinking about how she should ski, the more she kept herSELF from skiing. The same thing happens when you have a "mental block." The harder you keep thinking about what you should remember, the more you keep yourSELF from remembering. What do you do when you block your emotions? You keep your **emotions** from becoming **motions**. You don't let them move. The harder you keep thinking how you should feel, the more you keep yourSELF from feeling. Or, the moment you don't let your emotions move, you don't feel them. Emotional or "feeling" blocks then are really ways to keep yourSELF from feeling. If you feel pain and your suffering is real, but you don't feel the corresponding emotion, you are blocking it. You have a feeling block. Mental blocks, coordination blocks and feeling blocks are all energy blocks. They usually go hand in hand.

Energy blocks can keep you from remembering, from feeling and from moving. There is no motion. Something is blocking your motion. **You** are blocking your motion. One part of your energy wants to express itself through motion and another equal part of your energy tries to block this motion. You create the energy block yourself. Both the energy that seeks expression and the energy that blocks it are yours. Nothing moves. You have no energy available and you live under tension and in pain.

The skier's coordination block is an example of this. She kept her knees stiff. Her frustration really tired her out. Her pain was real when she hit the crossbar. The same holds true for feeling blocks. If you are angry at your mother, you feel resentment but think "nice" children shouldn't feel this way, so you block your feelings. Your resentment becomes emBODYed as an energy block in your body, say your jaw. You grind your teeth at night. You feel tension in your neck. You hurt, but you don't know how to get rid of it. Your energy is bound and there is no motion.

When you have Gestalt Body-Awareness, you allow for constant motion. When you move, you change. When you change, you grow. Every moment in your life is new. This is how change expresses itself in you. Sometimes it is very difficult to accept constant change. It becomes too threatening. You want to hold onto the status quo, to have control, control of yourSELF. Control makes you feel secure and precise. You think you can make things predictable. But all you do is create one energy block after another. Life changes constantly. The moment you allow yourself to change, to flow, and to go with your body energy, you "live dangerously." Only by living in this way can you continue to grow. Otherwise your whole life is one big energy block. And you are stuck.

THE THIRD ENERGY EXPLORATION

If you are able to make your body heavy and your center warm, you are ready to begin the third energy exploration. In this exploration you start out by saying the words: "I surrender mySELF" and then you repeat the key sentences from the first and the second energy explorations: "my body is heavy. my center is warm." At this point, you should actually be feeling the heaviness of your body and the warmth in your center. If you don't, you are not yet ready to begin the third exploration. You should go back and continue practicing the first two energy explorations until you get a feeling of heaviness in your body and a sense of warmth in your center.

The third energy exploration concentrates your awareness on your heart beat. In this exploration you explore the possibility of actually slowing down your pulse. A slower pulse along with the feelings of heaviness and warmth will bring you to a general feeling of inner relaxation and peace. This feeling prepares you to surrender yourSELF more easily and allows you to drift into the energy state more readily. Before you actually start, let me give you the words of the third energy exploration:

> I surrender mySELF
> my body is heavy
> my center is warm
>
> my pulse is calm
> my pulse is steady and calm
> my pulse is steady
> my pulse is calm
>
> I surrender mySELF
> my pulse is calm
>
> (Wait 30 seconds)

83

And then introduce the "coming out" routine, as you have done in the past. By now you are doing your energy explorations entirely alone. Perhaps you still work with your friend. Let me encourage you, either way.

Before you get started, I advise you and your friend to go through a supportive practice concerning the heart beat. First, take your friend's pulse. Put the three middle fingers of your left hand on the inside of your friend's right wrist just below the base of his thumb. Move your fingertips around and exert a slight pressure until you find the spot where you can feel his pulse best. See how many beats you

can count on your wristwatch within one minute. This will help you to develop a feeling for the rate of his heart beat. Now, let your friend take your pulse. When you are finished taking each other's pulse, both of you take your own pulse. To establish a criterion for your slowest pulse rate, take your own pulse immediately after you wake up in the morning, when you are in a naturally relaxed state.

Once you have a pretty good feeling for the rhythm of your heart beat, you and your friend can lie down on your backs together, close your eyes and try to experience the pulsation of your heart in your chests. This supportive practice will prepare you for the third energy exploration by giving you a feeling for the tempo of your heart. **Do not** concentrate on the pulse anywhere in your head — like around your temples or eyes. Stay below the neck.

By now each of you probably has a specific preference for how you do the energy explorations. Either you make yourselves **see** the words of the routine written across the dark sky of your closed eyes, you **hear** them in your head, or you **concentrate** on the voice of your agent. It doesn't matter how you do it, so long as it works for you. Sometimes it is helpful to continue experimenting with this a little bit on your own. This is partly why these sequences are called "explorations." Nothing really has to be. Everything is wide open. You try out a method and through your own experience find out what works best for you. Throughout your growth in GEBA Therapy you should always be open to new approaches. You might find that as you progress, your original opinions and preferences change. **The method is as open as you are.** For instance, you might be able to get your center warm by saying, "My center is green". Fine. In that case, you would replace my suggestive word "warm" with your word, "green", throughout the exploration. "My body is heavy; My center is green; My pulse is calm," etc. Whatever does the trick. You needn't bother to explain why this variation works for you. Who cares? You experience it and so you know it works. The word itself does not have to make sense. Learn to trust yourSELF.

TO MAKE SENSE IS NONSENSE. YOU ARE YOUR SENSES.

Now get ready to do the third energy exploration. Check your friend's position. Ask him to **close his eyes** and say to him in a calm voice:

I surrender mySELF
my body is heavy
my center is warm

my pulse is calm
my pulse is steady and calm
my pulse is steady
my pulse is calm

I surrender mySELF
my pulse is calm

(Wait 30 seconds)

my face is cool
my face is nice and cool
my face is cool

make fists
open your fists
take a deep breath
stretch out

(Wait 30 seconds)

open your eyes

By now your friend knows what he wants to tell you. Let him take over the verbal exchange portion of the exploration. Keep your suggestions to a minimum and wait with your questions and remarks until your friend has said all he wants to say. Perhaps he will be continuing an experience from his previous exploration, which arose again in a feeling just now. Clarify anything he talks about which you do not fully understand. Be sure that he can experience heaviness and warmth and that he is able to get in touch with his pulse. If he hasn't already spoken to you about them, you might now ask him the following additional questions.

Could you get in touch with your heart beat? Where could you pick up the pulse? Could you experience your pulse actually slowing down? Were there any other sensations that interfered with your concentrating on the pulsation? Was it a tranquil experience or did you feel anxious or agitated?

When your friend has said all he wants to and has opened his eyes, it may be time for you to change places, time for you to calm your pulse. Hand this book to your friend, and get on your way.

What you are aiming for, of course, is a slower pulse rate and an over-all relaxed mood. Once you can move into this exploration, beginning to calm your pulse, you are ready to focus on another aspect of energy exploration. Along with experiencing your heaviness, warmth, and slower pulse, you will begin to drift from time to time into the energy state. You will have to wait until the fifth week before you learn to work in this state. But you can start now to get more and more aware of the **quality** of that state. Allow yourSELF to drift and to discover the energy and the inner peace that becomes available to you. It is a beautiful feeling.

Practice the third energy exploration two or three times a day for a week or until you can really feel your heart beat slowing down and experience a calm pulsation through your whole body.

THE EXPERT GAME

Today people have become much more aware of the food they eat. They are beginning to listen to their bodies again. Of course, if you go on a natural food trip without listening to your body, you won't find anything miraculous in natural foods. You'll just be on another trip. The real importance behind the natural food trip is that you listen to your body; you eat what your body needs and you do not buy food for its package appearance or promises. I feel that when I eat too much red meat in the evening and haven't worked out physically enough during the day, the meal is just too heavy for me. Perhaps you also experience specific body sensations when you eat certain foods. If so, you are becoming your own expert by becoming more product-wise about nutrition and your body's needs.

The same is true for psychiatry, education and religion. If you don't rely on the "expert" to tell you what to eat, you definitely do not have to rely on the "expert" in the area of human conduct. The moment you do so you hand your body and thereby yourSELF over to someone else. You lose contact with yourself. If you feel upset and believe you're "going crazy," you head for an "expert." The moment you become a patient, you are **helpless** and the doctor is the **expert**. He has all the answers; he is going to cure you. This is the key to self-defeat! For in the role of the helpless patient, you are no longer responsible for yourself. You don't respond to yourself. You are dependent on another person and you must wait for them to do their "tricks" for you. Pills, chemo-therapy, electro-shock treatment, on-going "talk" shows are not going to do it for you.

Many people have confided to me that when they had a nervous breakdown, they reached a point where they could make the decision whether or not they would have the breakdown. This makes a lot of sense if you realize that **your body has the power to kill itself and to heal itself**. And above everything else, **you** are in charge of yourSELF, of your body. So when you go to the doctor and say "I am emotionally sick. I am mentally ill. Cure me," you have already given

up everything. You are merely waiting for the "expert" and the solutions to come to you. However, most of your problems of living cannot be solved by anyone else. Only you can change yourSELF. Only you can change the attitude behind your life.

The emphasis in GEBA Therapy is on your experience. Only you can experience your experience. The "answers" to your problems are definitely not in this book, or in my words. You have to do the experiencing and the living. You have to change your attitude so that you can grow as a person. I am not another expert, a doctor with all the answers acquired through years and years of academic study, nor are you the helpless creature who comes to me seeking a cure. In that setting, people who are treated for mental illness fall into the loser bracket. They can't possibly make it because the setting already works against them. Therefore, you are not anyone's patient; you are a student of life. Nobody can really solve your problems of living but yourself. Drugs, techniques and manipulations may give you temporary relief or may at best be supportive in certain instances, but in the long run the changing and the growing must be done by you.

GEBA Therapy gives you the tools to do your own growing. If you have **done** the book, you have used all of them already. Here they are:

1. **Supportive Practices:** By becoming aware of your level of tension (tonicity), you learn how to release yourSELF and by becoming aware of your manner of carriage (contact), you learn how to center yourSELF.

2. **Energy Explorations:** By being able to shift your awareness (spontaneity), you learn how to surrender yourSELF.

3.   **Sonance Explorations**: By working on the quality of your breathing (sonance), you learn how to integrate yourSELF.

With the help of these three tools, you learn to express GEstalt Body-Awareness and discover a new lifestyle attitude. When you can actually live GEBA during a large part of your everyday life, then you liberate yourSELF.

THE THIRD SONANCE EXPLORATION

Do you remember what I said about the breathing schedule for sonance explorations? It is only a general guideline for you and your friend to have something to go by as you start out. The actual amount of breathing that is done will have to be determined by your friend. Urge him to listen to himself from the very beginning and soon he will know when to stop and when to continue. The information comes from him. My arbitrary suggestion for the third sonance exploration is that you do two routines of up to fifty breathing cycles each. During the first fifty cycles, your friend will lie down on his stomach and you will do supportive practices on his calves and on his back while he is breathing. For the second fifty cycles, your friend will roll onto his back and you will put your hand on his center.

As you did in the last two weeks, you and your friend will again work on supportive practices first. Ask him to lie down on his stomach, to keep his arms at his sides, and to rest his head on either side. This will be the position each of you will assume during the first half of the third sonance exploration. While he is lying down like this, you will work on his calves and on his back.

Let's start with his calves. Put a pillow underneath his feet. A rolled-up blanket or a folded jacket can serve the same purpose. In this position his leg is not over-extended (stretched too far) and is more relaxed and easier to work on.

All the strokes in supportive practices move in the direction of the heart to support the bloodflow of the oxygen-poor blood back to the heart and to the lungs. The first sensation that usually occurs in the legs once full breathing begins is a tightness around the knees or a slight spasm in the lower legs. What you want to do if this should happen to your friend is to give him support in this area. The calves are big muscles and they are very good to work on with powerful, fluid strokes.

Sit or squat at your friend's foot and rub some oil on his left calf. Now stroke the calf muscles with one hand. First, let your fingers lead as you stroke; then turn your hand and let the outer edge of your hand lead as you stroke. Try to establish a complete contact with your

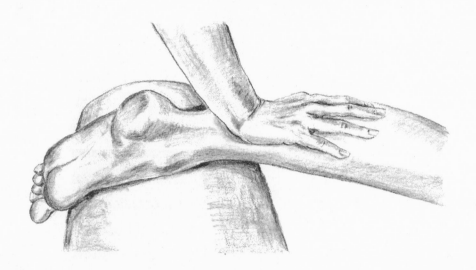

hand. Do about ten strokes. If you have too much oil on your hand, take some of it and rub your hand on his other calf. While you do this, be sure to maintain contact with your friend's calf with your other hand. Try never to break contact while you are doing a supportive practice. When you move your hands toward the heart, apply enough pressure to cause a squeezing action in the skin capillaries of the lower leg. The pressure should not be painful, but should get as close as possible to the pain threshold.

Next, let your middle finger ride on top of the calf muscle, squeezing it on the right side and the left side with your forefinger and your second finger respectively. Ten strokes are enough if you do them correctly. Now put both hands on either side of the right calf with

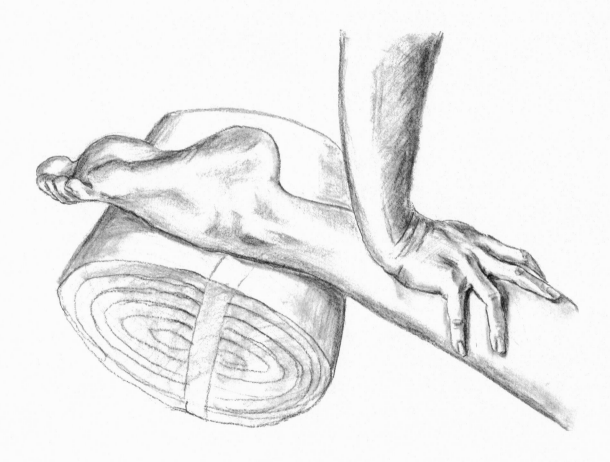

your thumbs spread out on top. Adjust your fingers to the form of his lower leg and push with your hands toward the back of his knee. Avoid

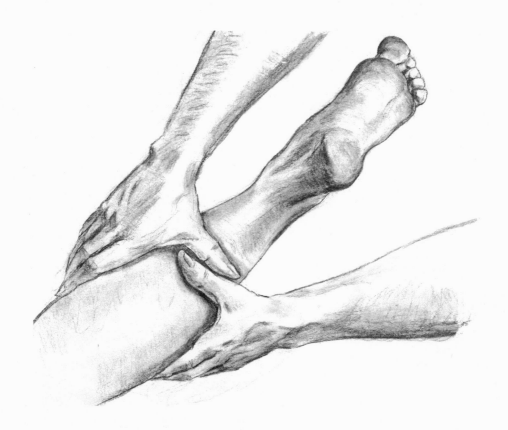

breaking contact. Just slide your hands back toward the knee, then ease up on the pressure as you return to the position from which you started. Then push again, exerting enough pressure to create a fluid and powerful rhythm. Experiment with these three different strokes. Eventually, you will find your own style and your own variations. But remember: always apply pressure toward the heart; don't break contact; try to find the right stroking speed.

The same rules hold true for kneading, the last supportive practice I want to teach you for the calves. Kneading is, as the name indicates, a continuous motion very much like kneading dough. Sit on your friend's right side. He should be still on his back, with his right lower leg in front of you. The pillow is still under his foot. Put your hands side by side across his calf with your thumbs toward you and your fingers reaching over the calf. Now lift the calf muscle slightly and let the clamps your fingers form with your thumbs work against each other. For this purpose your fingers and your thumb form a V; then you work one hand against the other thumb. This way your right thumb presses against the fingers of your left hand and your left thumb presses against the fingers of your right hand. You start on the bottom

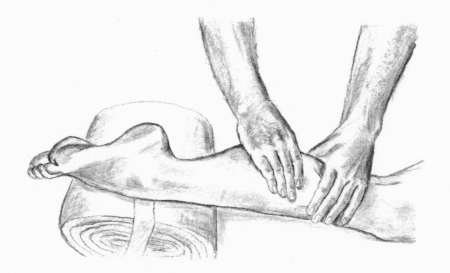

of the calf muscle and work toward the back of the knee. At the knee you return to your original position again and continue to knead the muscle as before. Back and forth, one hand against the other.

Finish working on the right calf by stroking it several times as you did in the beginning of the practice. Then switch over to the other calf. Stroke this leg first with one hand, then with both hands, knead the calf muscle, and finish the entire supportive practice by stroking the whole calf. During the sonance exploration you can allow about two minutes for each calf muscle.

Prepare your friend for the three-part backstroke by putting a pillow underneath his chest. By draping his upper body over the pillow, you provide room for him to turn his head sideways and to relax his neck and shoulder muscles. The pillow also acts as a comfortable cushion for a woman's breasts. Tell your friend to keep his arms at his sides. Apply some oil to his back in a circular motion. Put both of your hands on his lower back, one on either side of the vertebrae. Your thumbs go together and your fingers are parallel. Now ask your friend to accentuate his breathing so you can pick up his breathing rhythm with your hands by looking at his back. Inhale deeply and exhale. The moment he is on top of an inhalation, start stroking toward his neck with both of your hands. During this upward stroke, each hand is on one side of the vertebrae until your fingers reach both sides of the neck. This first part of the stroke coincides with your friend's exhalation which you support with strong pressure on his back. At the end of the exhalation, let your right hand sweep across your friend's right shoulder and your left hand sweep across the left shoulder. This second part of the stroke should coincide with the pause between his exhalation and his next inhalation. During the third part of the back stroke, you mold your friend's sides with both of your hands, with your fingers spread far apart. Your friend inhales during this motion, as your hands meet again on the bottom of his lower back. Then the whole routine can start again. In sum, the three-part back stroke goes like this: One — Your friend exhales while you press down your hands and push toward his neck. Two — He pauses and you sweep around across the shoulders. Three — He inhales while you slide your hands back down his sides to their original position. This is a good way for

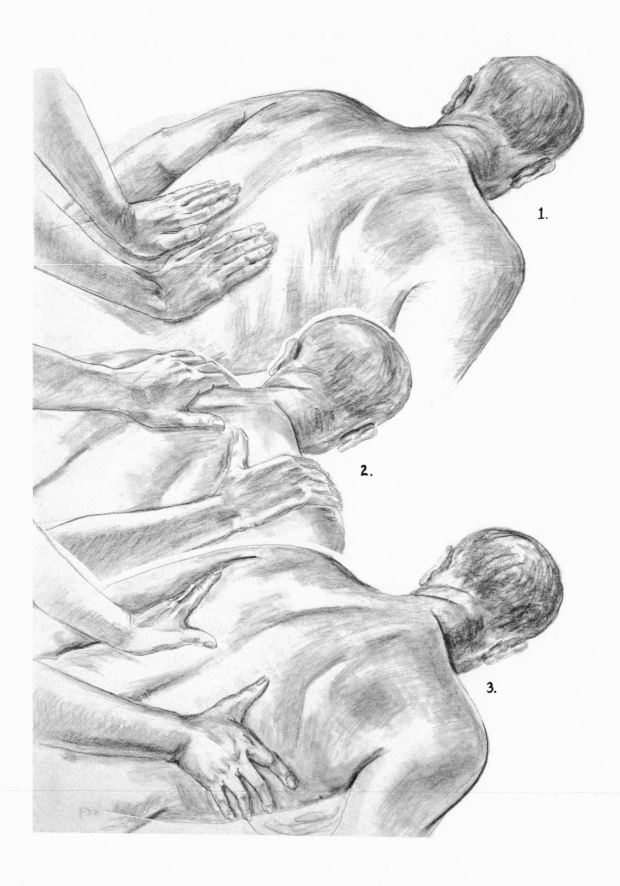

1.

2.

3.

you to tune in to his breathing cycle, which will be important when you support him during the actual sonance exploration. You should allow three to four minutes for working on the three-part backstroke. After some practice you will develop a smooth and rhythmical motion and increase your ability to judge exactly how hard to press during the first part of the stroke.

Now, change places and give your friend a chance to work on your calves and on your back. This gives you a chance to experience both parts of the practice. Pay attention to yourself. You will gain valuable information not only as an explorer but also as an agent.

For the third sonance exploration I advise your friend to undress completely or at most just wear a light pair of shorts. The more his body is exposed, the easier it will be to do the supportive practices and the easier it is to observe him. Ask him to lie down while you put one pillow under his feet and another under his chest. Tell him that he will be breathing fifty breathing cycles while lying on his stomach. For the second half of this exploration he will turn over onto his back again and breathe a second fifty. While he is lying on his stomach, you will do your supportive practices on his calves and legs. Now start out the usual way by establishing contact with your friend. This time, you put your hand on his lower back. Tell him to **close his eyes** and start to

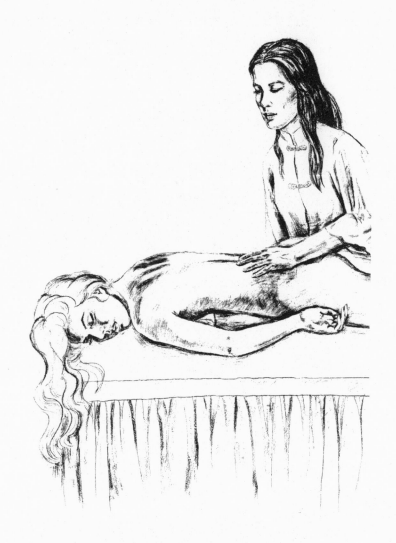

pay attention to his breathing. Once you feel he is in touch with his breathing, tell him to wet his lips, drop his jaw, and start inhaling and exhaling through his mouth. His deep breathing should stay the same but his head is tilted sideways, resting on one side with his mouth open. Whenever he is ready, he should start breathing deeply through his mouth, and sighing ... Ahhhhhhhh on the exhalation.

Now you can begin your supportive practices. Work two minutes on the right calf, two minutes on the left calf and three to four minutes on the back. It should take you about as long as it will take your friend to finish his fifty breathing cycles. Remind him to keep his eyes closed throughout the procedure. When you come close to the end of your supportive practice, tell him:

> Two more deep breaths. Inhale and exhale. Inhale and release yourself. Very good. Now switch to breathing regularly through your nose. Lie still for thirty seconds and pay attention to yourself.

After the time has past, tell your friend to turn over on his back. Remove the pillows and reestablish contact with your friend by putting your hand on his center. Look into your friend's face. It always amazes me how people look so much younger after this sonance exploration. They have a natural flush to their face which gives them a very youthful appearance. If everything seems all right, ask your friend to start with his second set of fifty breathing cycles. Tell him that this time he should tune in to himSELF and "fish" for emotions behind the sensations he experiences. Remember: Sensations are tingling, numbness, twitching, buzzing, and similar feelings like itching of the skin, or feeling a cool breeze on some part of the body. Emotions are resentment, joy, sadness, anger, guilt, grief, etc. If he feels comfortable enough with these feelings, encourage him to go with them. Sometimes they might evolve as feelings of sensuality. If he feels a vibrating in his genitals and lower abdomen, ask him to go with the sensation and to explore the sexual feeling that might follow. Tell him that it's all right. Let him try to allow himSELF to be horny!

All of your talking during the exploration and the verbal exchange after the exploration are part of the supportive practice. We began in the second week to let your friend take over the verbal exchange. Now encourage him to take over more and more until he gets the feeling that he is running the show. If he's breathing and everything seems all right, "let it be." If he doesn't feel comfortable, by now he knows when to stop. Just stay in contact with your friend and keep your hand on his center. Your hand contact tells him that everything is all right with you. But the rest from here on out will be more and more up to him. During this time you can pay more attention to your own feelings.

In case any kind of emotion should start to surface in your friend, only he will know if it is spontaneous, genuine, and if he feels a need to express it. So, for instance, if he feels joyful or amused and he starts laughing, it's all right. It is important that your friend knows that nothing is really expected of him. He should just listen to himself and whatever occurs in his body, he should get in touch with and try to follow. So, first he gets in touch with sensations, then he gets in touch with emotions, then he allows these emotions to surface, and by letting them surface, he will express them by acting them out. After his second set of fifty breathing cycles, again ask your friend to slow down and switch to breathing through his nose. Ask him to put his awareness into his body. Tell him to wait for about thirty seconds like he did after the first part of this exploration. Then ask him to open his eyes and share his experiences with you. When your friend is finished reporting what he felt and feels, it might be helpful for you to express your own feelings to your friend. Did you as the agent feel comfortable? Did you feel suddenly that you were responsible for your friend? Did you feel anxious yourself? Don't forget, responsibility really is the ability for you to respond to yourself. All you have to do is give your friend a chance to respond to himself. You are so used to taking "responsibilities" for others that you become very manipulative and find it difficult to give up your controls over others, find it difficult to leave them alone.

Here is an example of a subtle control that can be exerted over another person in the name of "responsibility": I tell my wife that as her husband I feel responsible for her safety and therefore I don't want her to drive alone into New York City. But if I were truly responding to myself, I would know that the real reason I don't want her to drive into the city is my fear that if she should get too independent, I might lose her. As long as I know **how** I am really restricting her, I can remain in pretty good shape. But it really gets bad when I actually see myself as the white knight who acts only in her best interest. Because then I am not only controlling her, but I am also controlling mySELF! Are you a white knight?

Now, switch places with your friend and begin your own sonance exploration.

As an arbitrary measure, I suggest that you do this third sonance exploration three times every second day during the week. Practice the energy exploration two or three times each day. And at this point, you might be comfortable enough to do both of them alone. If you don't feel comfortable alone or if you just prefer to have somebody with you, as many people do, continue to work with your agent.

LIFE IS FOR YOU TO EXPLORE
YOUR WAY IS UNTOUCHED
NO ONE HAS BEEN THERE BEFORE.

THE PERFORMANCE SYNDROME

During the past year, I have had more people "scream" in my practice than ever before. They read somewhere that screaming will cure them, so at the first opportunity they have, they scream. I call this the **performance syndrome** or "what you think is what you get." If you scream just because you think you should scream, you keep yourself from ever being able to really scream. In other words, you never scream spontaneously. You think you should scream, so you scream. But you (your body) may not be ready to scream or has no need to scream at all. In this case, by screaming you cover up all kinds of spontaneous stuff that could come up if you would leave yourself alone. So, leave yourself alone. Listen to yourSELF. Listen to your body and let whatever emerges happen spontaneously. If you feel sad, go with your sadness. If tears come into your eyes, let yourself cry. If you feel angry and need to express it, act on your anger in your own way. Only you know if your feelings and their expressions are spontaneous or if they are **performed**.

Look at this woman. She seems self-assured and gives the appearance that she likes what she sees in the mirror. But is this really

so? Only she knows. If her posture is the true emBODYment of her feelings, then I call her motion a **gesture**. If this posture is a cover for her feelings of insecurity and inadequacy, then I call her motion a **performance**.

In GEBA Therapy you work with gestures. You try to stay true to yourSELF. You try never to manipulate any one into an emotional outburst. And that includes yourSELF. So, if you put a specific value on screaming, you only keep another person or yourself from screaming spontaneously. If you think you should scream, the chances are that you will scream, but your organism may not feel like screaming. And the same is true about all emotions and their expressions. It is all right to cry, to scream, to laugh, to get angry as long as they are gestures. Many people have a lot of joy buried inside of them. If you do and you express this joy, you will have a primal laugh. And as I have said before, once emotions surface and are acted upon, it is not necessary to try to explain them. The solution is in the experience. They occur spontaneously while you get in touch with them. You experience HOW and then you **know**. You don't have to explain WHY any more.

YOU ARE YOUR BODY.
THE MORE YOU HAVE TO EXPLAIN
WHO YOU ARE,
THE MORE YOU ARE NO-BODY.

THE SOBER HIGH

You are plugged into a bigger energy field than just your body's — the energy field of nature. And when you are tuned in well to this energy field, you say you are healthy. If you are in discord within, then you speak of dis-ease. The struggle, therefore, is not **against** disease, but **for** health. It is not sickness that interfers with your lifestyle, but rather your **abortive lifestyle** that makes you sick. You have to surrender to nature, to your nature in order to survive. If you move too far away from nature, you live an abortive life-style and your body reacts to it by getting "sick." So instead of listening to nature, to your nature, you are in conflict with it. And when you are in conflict with your nature, you are in conflict with yourSELF. You are in pain. You have no body-energy. So your body really becomes your weak part, the part of you that is denied, controlled, supressed, and a source of pain and embarrassment. Instead of being a source of pleasure and spontaneity, your body becomes only the transportation system for your head. You cover it up. You ignore your body or deal with it just like any other object. You weigh it. You wash it. You put it on a diet. You use it to conquer somebody else. Your body becomes a tool. It is not something you can enjoy; it is just something you use.

But your body does have its own life, its energy, its vivacity, its vigor, its gestures, its feelings, and the power to heal itself. Your body is **you** expressing your energy within a larger energy field. You charge, you discharge, you inhale, you exhale, you experience power, and you experience pleasure. If you don't give up your power, if you "hold on," you stop the energy flow in your body and you can't experience pleasure. So there you are, up and tight, unable to experience pleasure,

unable to relax. You can't swing. You give off bad vibrations. You are blocked. There are energy vibrations all around you but you don't go with these vibrations. Everything around you is changing but you keep yourself from changing by blocking your energy. This blocked energy is not a mystical thing. It is something you can see. Just look at people. Look at their eyes. Look at how their eyes are filled with tears, with sadness, with depression, with fear, with surprise, how their voice goes up and down, or how they speak only in a monotone. Look at their skin. Is it alive or is it dead and grayish? Look at their movements. Do they move as though they have energy, as if they know where they are going? If your body is a mess, no matter how sharp your intelligence may be, you are no-BODY. You have no spontaneity; you aren't moving. You aren't living.

It is important that you rediscover your nature, rid yourself of tension and provide yourSELF with energy for living. Whenever your body energy becomes one with the energy field of the universe, you experience a rare moment of ecstasy in your life. I call this moment the **sober high.** You can experience the sober high many different ways, as long as it is a true gesture of your organism: dancing, playing a musical instrument, giving birth, skiing, any kind of motion. Thinking can be as beautiful as the work of your hands when it is spontaneous.

I'm a skier and have skied all my life. One of the sober highs I remember is being in two feet of powder snow and at one with the sky. Just bombing the mountain without having to prove anything, I no longer knew that I had skis on my feet. It is the same kind of feeling as when you are in love and you lose all sense of time. You are absorbed by the moment. During these episodes of total surrender, you are high on your own energy rather than on the energy of some outside source — like booze, drugs, or any form of manipulation. You surrender yourSELF and thereby gain the ultimate in living, the **sober high**.

When water is scooped up by the hands,
the moon is reflected in them;
when flowers are handled,
the scent soaks into the robe.

Wu-tsu Fa-yen

THE FOURTH WEEK

THE HEAD TRIP

When your body is right here but your awareness is in the future, you are anticipating. When your body is here but your awareness is in the past, you are reminiscing. Either way you have a Body Awareness Split (BAS). This attitude prevents you from being involved in **doing** because you are busy **thinking** about what you should do or what you could have done. Relief from a situation like this can come only through doing. But you can't do anything about it right now because it hasn't happened yet, might never happen, or has already happened. In other words, **your body is alarmed about what you think, but can't act on it**. You are on a head trip. Whenever you are on a head trip you are anticipating; you are anxious. You put your body under mental stress and emotional tension. Your body becomes the victim of your head. You can't keep yourSELF from thinking: "Will the deal work out tomorrow?" "Why do I keep going around and around in my head?" "Why did she do this to me?" "Why can't I sleep?" "What will the neighbors think?" "If only I had done this instead of that." "Why can't I stop worrying?" While all this thinking about tomorrow and yesterday is going on in your head, your body keeps preparing itself to move but no motion ever takes place. The head is somewhere else and has lost contact with the body. The body is treated just like another object. The body is suffering. The suffering is real and the body is you.

So, if the headtrip takes over and you stop listening to your body, then your body hurts and you experience pain. And after your body experiences enough pain, unfortunately you think up another headtrip of how to repair what you have already damaged. In other words, you live an abortive lifestyle which causes your body to go to pieces. And then instead of changing your attitude and thereby your abortive lifestyle, you find another headtrip to repair what went to pieces and brought the whole thing about to begin with. Let me give you an example. If you have a nervous breakdown, you don't have it from one day to the next. You get many warnings from your body like: insomnia, constipation, ulcers, migraine headache, lack of energy, chest pains, hypertension, etc. But your head is so "strong" that it overrules your body messages until it is finally too late and you fall completely apart. Then you have the infamous "nervous breakdown" which is really the only **healthy** alternative the body has left — short of total collapse and death. And so this last healthy plea from your body is called a sickness and the second phase of your eternal headtrip begins. You call in the "experts" and become the helpless patient. And from here the psycho-circus begins — with all the "cures" from drugs to electro-shock.

But treating the symptoms will not solve your problem. You must go beyond the symptoms — to your attitude. If you only treat the symptoms, your headtrip continues. Therefore, in order to really bring about change, you have to listen to your body, to your nature. You must unite your awareness with your body. When you are on a headtrip, you do just the opposite. You spend much of your energy just keeping your headtrip going and an equal amount of energy defending your body against your headtrip. All previously mentioned warning signals are in fact energy manifestations used to defend the body. This energy is diametrically opposed to the energy used to carry out your headtrip. You can imagine how much of your energy is wasted in this inner conflict. You are in a mess but you blame your body for getting "sick." But it is not your body that makes you sick. Your body is your nature and nature is neutral and shameless. What makes you "sick" is the perversion of your head — your headtrip.

THE ENERGY STATE

During the first three energy explorations you concentrated on specific sensations in different areas of your body. You put your awareness in the service of your body in order to experience heaviness, warmth, and the calming of your pulse. The moment you can do this successfully, you **know** that you have GEstalt Body-Awareness. Without this lifestyle attitude you could not experience these body sensations. Now that your awareness is united with your body, you can surrender yourSELF even further and allow yourSELF to drift into a state which lies somewhere between being awake and being asleep. This experience I call the energy state. By shifting from the awakened state into the energy state, you shift from an attitude of having your body split from your awareness to an attitude in which you surrender your awareness to your body. There are as many descriptions of the energy state as there are people who can get into it. Here are some of them: "I felt like levitating." "This is how it must have been back in the womb." "I experienced my body moving out of my body." "It is like floating in the ocean." "A religious experience." "At no other time am I more at peace and one with the universe."

The truth is that the energy state can never be adequately described. Neither can I tell you **why** it happens. All I can do is show you **how** you can experience it. Once you experience it, you **know** what it is.

Let me summarize the whole process for you:

1. You practice the energy explorations (for instance, "my center is warm").

2. Through practice you are able to put your awareness (warmth) into your body (center).

3. By uniting your awareness with your body, you begin to drift into the energy state.

4. You know when you are in the energy state. It is a feeling between being awake and being asleep. You also experience the attitude which is basic to the energy state.

5. This attitude is GEstalt Body-Awareness. The energy state helps you to become familiar with this attitude and vice versa.

6. Once you **know** this attitude in the energy state, you can begin to use it in the awakened state by actually living GEstalt Body-Awareness in everyday life.

The main value the energy state has for GEBA Therapy is that it provides you with the actual experience of GEstalt Body-Awareness. Without this attitude you can't get into the energy state. Also, by surrendering yourSELF, you can use the energy state as a tool for general relaxation and energy recharge. In addition, I will introduce you next week to different exciting explorations you can do while you are in the energy state.

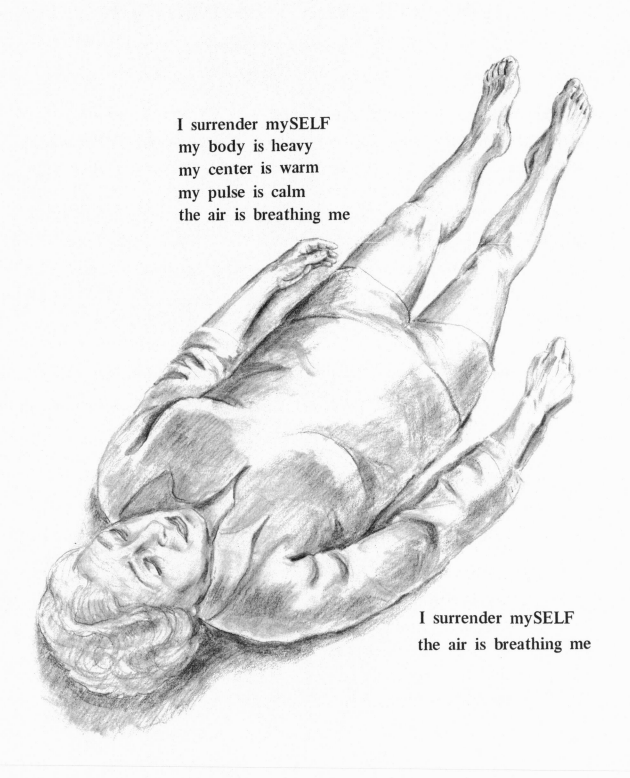

I surrender mySELF
my body is heavy
my center is warm
my pulse is calm
the air is breathing me

I surrender mySELF
the air is breathing me

THE FOURTH ENERGY EXPLORATION

Before introducing your friend to the fourth energy exploration, be sure that he can experience heaviness in his body, warmth in his center and a calm pulse. If he is unable to achieve one of the above experiences, continue to practice the respective energy exploration with him. Once he can fully experience the body sensations that go with "my body is heavy," "my center is warm," and "my pulse is calm," he is ready to take the next step.

The fourth energy exploration has been designed to assist your friend in drifting deeper and deeper into the energy state. The energy state, as I have pointed out before, provides your friend with:

1.   the actual experience of GEBA
2.   a tool for relaxation and recharge
3.   an opportunity for further explorations.

Here is the verbal structure for the fourth energy exploration:

> I surrender mySELF
> my body is heavy
> my center is warm
> my pulse is calm
>
> the air is breathing me
> the air is breathing me
> the air is breathing me
> the air is breathing me
>
> I surrender mySELF
> the air is breathing me

As you can see, your friend begins this exploration by repeating the key sentences of the first three energy explorations. After that you present to him the sentence "the air is breathing me." By repeating the routine four times he should be able to drift deeper into the energy state. You present the last two lines to him only once. From then on it is up to him to repeat "I surrender mySELF," "the air is breathing me" as many times as he wants to.

The actual shift into the energy state can start at any point along the routine. In fact, it happens to different people at different times. Some begin to drift the moment they say the first sentence, "I surrender mySELF." Others wait until they get to "the air is breathing me" before shifting into the energy state. Tell your friend:

> In case you have difficulty getting into the energy state, keep repeating "I surrender mySELF, the air is breathing me, I surrender mySELF, the air is breathing me" over and over again. The repetition of the last two lines at the end of the fourth energy exploration has a mantra-like effect. It will help you to surrender yourSELF more and more. You will know when you reach that space. As you go along you will also develop a feeling for the quality of the energy state on the basis of your own experience.

The "coming out routine" remains the same as before:

> My face is cool
> my face is nice and cool
> my face is cool

make fists
open your fists
take a deep breath
stretch out

(wait 30 seconds)

open your eyes

The only difference is that **he** will decide when to come out and will do so on his own. The first sign you will get from him that he is terminating the energy exploration will be when he "makes fists." Tell your friend that after he is finished with the coming out routine to wait again thirty seconds before opening his eyes.

Let's get started. The positions are the same as before. So after you and your friend are ready, you can introduce him to the fourth energy exploration:

I surrender mySELF
my body is heavy
my center is warm
my pulse is calm

the air is breathing me
the air is breathing me
the air is breathing me
the air is breathing me

I surrender mySELF
the air is breathing me

From here on he is on his own. You wait quietly until he opens his eyes. After that you can establish hand contact with him and wait for him to share his experiences with you. Keep **your** talking to a minimum. Instead, tune in and really listen to your friend. Talk only when you feel whatever he says about his experience could be enhanced. Otherwise, don't interfere. Let it be. The responsibility is solely with him. Give him the opportunity to respond to himSELF. This is where all the emphasis should be. If you work alone, continue to record your explorations in your journal or on a tape.

The fourth energy exploration, like all the others, should be practiced regularly twice a day until the desired feeling of "the air is breathing me" and the drifting into the energy state can be experienced. This exploration is the key routine for getting deeper and quicker into the energy state.

THE ALARM REACTION

The **alarm reaction** has a very important function in your life when you confront real conflict or danger. It prepares your body to take immediate action, enabling you to run away or to attack. If it happens to be a false alarm, your organism automatically returns to its normal state.

It is different when you are on a headtrip. The danger does not exist in reality. It only exists in your head. You anticipate what could happen if . . . but your body can't act on it. It can only **react** to your headtrip. In its natural function, the alarm reaction is of very short duration. It prepares you to act. The activated energy is discharged immediately through your action. The headtrip, on the other hand, can continue for prolonged periods of time. You anticipate and anticipate and anticipate and your body reacts and reacts and reacts but you never act. Some people live their whole lives like this. Their energy is **bound** and they experience constant tension.

You can get a pretty good feeling for the alarm reaction by pretending to be suddenly surprised by a dangerous situation. Act startled as though you were pantomiming a frightening situation. Now get in touch with what happens to your body. The first reaction you probably become aware of is that you suck air in and stop breathing. You shoulders are pulled up and you are probably up on your toes with your pelvis rigid and your legs stiff. You are up and you are tight.

Now let me show you what happens to you if this alarm reaction continues for a prolonged period of time, when general body tension turns into a chronic state. Your brows are pulled together. The muscles of your eyes and forehead are tight. Your eyes are wide open and the pupils are dilated. There's a worried look on your face. Your tongue is coated. Your mouth is dry and your lips are pursed. You feel a tenseness in your jaw as though you had a lump in your throat. You are choking. The muscles of your neck and throat are tense. You are holding on to your breath and breathing shallow. The emphasis is on the inhalation. You hold your breath, which gives you a feeling of control and power. But the holding on only makes your chest immobile and pulls your shoulders up. Your arms assume a defensive position. Your hands are over-extended and cold and sweaty. Your pelvis is rigid. Your anus is pulled in. You are up on your toes. Your genitals are contracted. You are up and tight.

What is showing on the outside of your body is only the result of what is going on inside of you. Have a look: your larynx is tightening up. You can hear it by the way you speak and breathe. Your blood vessels are constricted and your heart rate is increased. Your blood pressure is rising. Your adrenal cortex reacts with over-secretion and provides for continuous hypertension. This way even without actual stress, you keep your blood pressure up, produce chronic muscular tension and upset your blood sugar level (reactive hypoglycemia). The spasm of the sphincter muscles of your stomach keeps air from passing through. The air starts collecting in your stomach. Your stomach balloons. Your heart is pushed up. You feel pressure on your heart and butterflies in your stomach. Because your heart is pushed up, the left side of your lungs is compressed. You feel pain and tension on your left side. Your diaphragm is raised and rigid and cannot swing freely. Your breathing is shallow. The tightening of your anus causes constipation, anal itching, and hemorrhoids. The increased acidity in your stomach gives you peptic ulcers. The tenseness in your jaw makes you grind your teeth at night. Your over-worked head answers with a migraine. You are one big energy block. You are in pain. You are hurting.

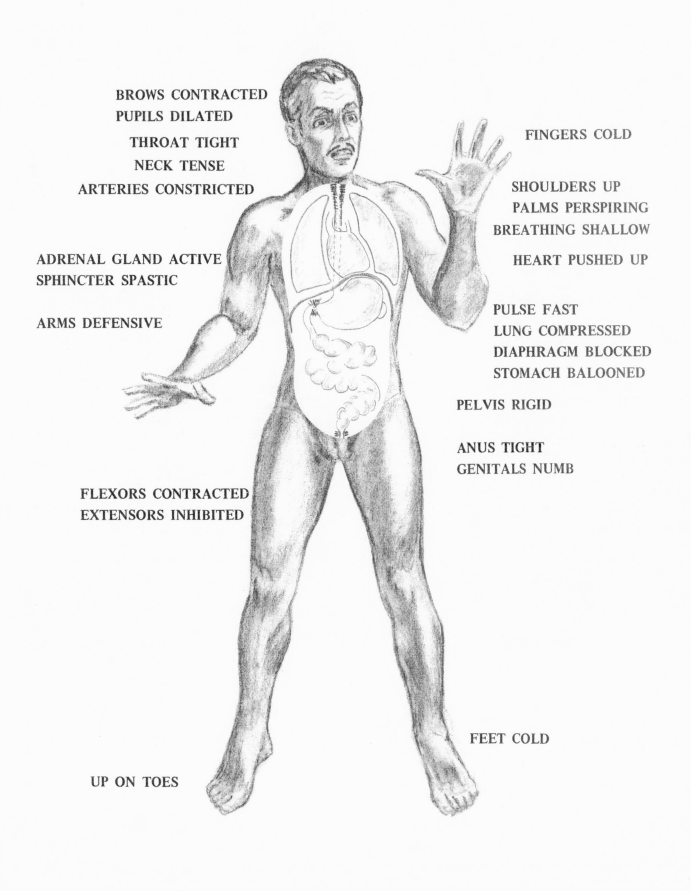

BROWS CONTRACTED
PUPILS DILATED
THROAT TIGHT
NECK TENSE
ARTERIES CONSTRICTED

ADRENAL GLAND ACTIVE
SPHINCTER SPASTIC

ARMS DEFENSIVE

FLEXORS CONTRACTED
EXTENSORS INHIBITED

UP ON TOES

FINGERS COLD

SHOULDERS UP
PALMS PERSPIRING
BREATHING SHALLOW

HEART PUSHED UP

PULSE FAST
LUNG COMPRESSED
DIAPHRAGM BLOCKED
STOMACH BALOONED

PELVIS RIGID

ANUS TIGHT
GENITALS NUMB

FEET COLD

Well, what can you do to get out from this dilemma? The usual way to escape this hypertense state is to collapse completely. This shift from one extreme to another is most commonly accomplished through booze, drugs, health gadgets, manipulations, or simply by falling apart. For instance, the "T.G.I.F." (Thank God it's Friday) syndrome illustrates this point. You work all week, worrying, anticipating, fretting and hassling and on Friday at 5:00 you "let down" with about three double martinis, or whatever works for you. After a few drinks you've eliminated all sensations of tension by knocking yourself out. You're collapsed. But neither in the state of hypertension nor in the state of collapse are you really relaxed. That is, both conditions prevent you from truly experiencing yourSELF. Your senses are dulled and distorted. You "think" you are relaxed.

Treating the symptoms of an abortive lifestyle can only bring temporary relief. If your attitude is wrong, you are living an abortive lifestyle and are paying a high price for it. Is it worth it? The alarm state which once was your protector has become your enemy — your state of permanent tension.

BODY ENERGY AND SONANCE

In the beginning of the book I told you that sonance explorations help you to integrate energy into every part of your body. You began this process by breathing and by concentrating on a variety of sensations. After some time you were able to recognize a specific sensation which could be described as a buzzing, a streaming, an "electrical" feeling or a high-frequency vibration. When you discover these vibrations in an area of your body, you are sonant or you have sonance in that respective body zone.

What you are actually feeling is the motion of energy in your body. Energy is available to you. The opposite is happening when you have no feelings or when you feel numb, cold, or tense. In this case energy is bound, creating energy blocks in your body. Then energy ceases to be available.

Energy, as I have said before, expresses itself through your body in the form of sensations, emotions or motions, which are themselves complex plasmatic, tonic, electrical or chemical movements. The functioning of these energy currents can only be partially explained. You must experience them! And sonance explorations are one way to do it. For instance: if you are sonant around your mouth, let the vibrations spread into your throat. There is really nothing you have to understand about this process. As a matter of fact I cannot explain it to you. All I can do is show you **how** to get there. You start with breathing; you get in touch with sensations; you fish for high-frequency vibrations in your body; you discover them in one area of your body; you then **know** what it is to be sonant in that specific body zone. Through practice you are able to turn the sonance vibrations on and off or shift them into adjacent areas, or **body zones** as I call them. Eventually, you can get your body sonant all over. Here is a body zone chart which will help you to orient yourself to this work:

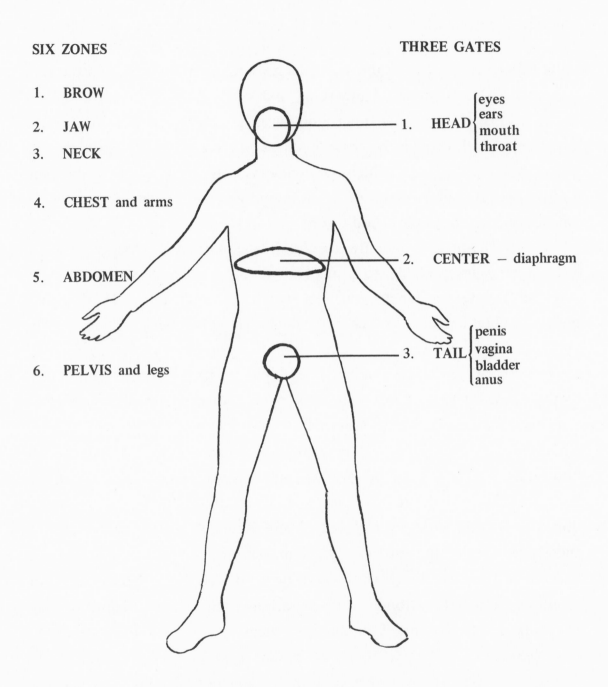

SIX ZONES

1. BROW

2. JAW

3. NECK

4. CHEST and arms

5. ABDOMEN

6. PELVIS and legs

THREE GATES

1. HEAD $\begin{cases} \text{eyes} \\ \text{ears} \\ \text{mouth} \\ \text{throat} \end{cases}$

2. CENTER – diaphragm

3. TAIL $\begin{cases} \text{penis} \\ \text{vagina} \\ \text{bladder} \\ \text{anus} \end{cases}$

In case you do not have any sensations in certain parts of your body or all you can feel is tension, numbness or spasm, continue to practice the sonance explorations. Through breathing and with the help of the supportive practices for the respective body zones, continue to work toward opening up your energy blocks. Follow the sensation, emotion and motion chain. The processes of your being sonant (sensation), of letting your feelings surface (emotion) and of actually expressing your feelings (motion) go hand in hand. You gain insight by practicing the sonance explorations — by doing. Nobody can explain these experiences to you. You experience and then you **know**.

Bottled up emotions create energy blocks in different body areas. But there are no fixed rules that a tight jaw, for instance, stands for anger. This is a pre-judgment. It just might be that this is the way you keep yourSELF from talking. The same is true about other attempts at categorizing people. Whether you are an anal or oral character, a neurotic or a schizophrenic (depending on the system you follow), the fact remains that these are only names. And these names will stand in the way of your changing yourSELF. These headtrips might sound very interesting and the analysis might be fascinating, but the answer is in you and not in their systems of thought.

By being able to be sonant, you have a tool to experience the energy flow in your body and to recognize energy blocks. Through sonance exploration you discover where they are, what they are and how to dissolve them. You integrate yourSELF. Once your energy blocks are dissolved, your tension vanishes, body energy becomes available to you, and **you have sonance**.

THE FOURTH SONANCE EXPLORATION

As in the previous weeks, you and your friend start out with several supportive practices first. This time you will work on your friend's thighs and on his chest. Remember, the order in which I present these supportive practices is arbitrary. From here on out you will use them during the sonance exploration whenever a situation calls for them. That is, when your friend tells you he has no sensations in a certain body zone or if he feels tension, numbness, or cold.

Ask your friend to lie down on his back and put a pillow underneath his knees. This way his leg muscles will not be over-stretched and when you put pressure on them he will feel no pain on the underside of his legs. Also, when his legs are bent, they are more relaxed and you can reach underneath them better when you are working on the inside or outside of his thigh. The supportive practices for his thighs are much the same as you used on his calves. Start out by stroking his right thigh with both hands from just above the knee to where the leg joins the pelvis. Your hands are on either side of the thigh with the thumbs spread out on top. Have your fingers adjust to the form of the upper leg and apply pressure as you stroke toward the heart.

Don't break contact when you let your hands slide back. Ease up on the pressure until you return to the place above the knee from where you can start the next stroke. Use a fluid and powerful motion.

The next supportive practice is very much like the kneading motion you used on his calves. This time you will be working on the inside of his thigh. Stand on your friend's right side when you are working on the inside of his right thigh. This way your friend's leg will be between your body and your hands. Put both hands next to each other on the inside of your friend's thighs. Your thumbs are on top and the fingers are toward the under side of his thighs. Lift his muscles slightly away from his thigh bone and let the clamps your fingers form with your thumb work against each other. The pressure in this grip is mainly applied with the thumbs against the fingers of the other hand.

Start out with both hands close to the knee. With a continuous and powerful rhythm, very much like kneading dough, you work all the way up to his crotch. Again avoid breaking contact and slide with both hands back to the inside of the knee. Then start again to knead the thighs all the way to his crotch. After kneading the inside of the thigh several times, finish off by stroking his thigh with your right hand.

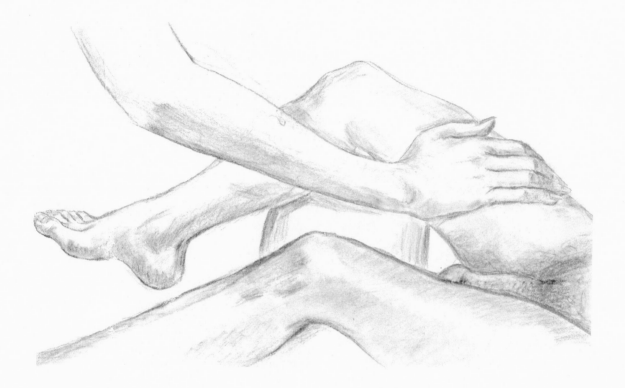

The same procedure should be repeated with the left thigh. Once you have stroked and kneaded both thighs, stand at his feet and put your right hand with the fingers spread on top of his right thigh and your left hand with the fingers spread on top of his left thigh. Now start stroking both sides at the same time and apply quite a bit of pressure with both hands. Keep your arm straight while doing this. Find a soothing and powerful rhythm which is not too fast and not too slow.

The next supportive practice you start by stroking your friend's chest with one hand from the center part of the sternum toward the area below his clavicle. Use fairly rapid circular strokes with your thumb on one side of the sternum and your forefinger and middle finger on the other side of it. Exert quite a bit of pressure. You can

perform this stroking of the chest while sitting next to your friend, since the motion only involves your underarm, your wrist, and your hand.

For the next supportive practice, which I call the chest pump, stand behind your friend's head. Put both hands on his chest. Spread your fingers wide apart with your palms just below the clavicle. Adjust to your friend's breathing cycle for a moment, then press down hard with each exhalation. By watching your friend you will get a feeling for

how much force you should apply. Tell him to yield to your pressure. Working with your friend for about ten breaths this way will be sufficient. Now change places and give your friend a chance to work on you.

The arbitrary time limit for the fourth sonance exploration is one hundred breathing cycles, or about fifteen minutes of breathing. Let me repeat again: this measure is arbitrary. The emphasis is not on the amount of breathing your friend can do, but on the sensations and feelings he can allow himself to express.

During the first half of the fourth sonance exploration, ask your friend to concentrate on sensations and to "fish" for high-frequency vibrations in his body. While his awareness is with his body sensations, he can report these sensations to you without interrupting his breathing too much. If he feels numb, tense, cold, or tells you that he has no feeling in a specific body zone, do the respective supportive practice for that area.

During the second half of the sonance exploration, encourage your friend to direct his awareness toward emotions like anger, resentment, joy, sadness, etc. If he is able to tune into certain feelings, he should try to let his emotions surface by letting his feelings move him. There is no predescribed form for the movement that emerges. Joy, for instance, could bring about a smile, laughter, or slapping one's thighs. Resentment could result in crying, hitting, kicking, swearing, or just talking about it. Sadness could result in being absolutely quiet, in getting restless, in starting to sob. Just tell your friend to follow his feelings and to let his feelings move him. In whatever form these movements emerge, it's all right. There is really nothing he has to do. It is better to do nothing at all than to try and force some preconceived pattern on himself. During the second half of the fourth sonance exploration, you as the agent, should keep your own talking to an absolute minimum. Just keep your hand on his center, go with him, and prepare him in the beginning that you are not going to say very much. Don't forget, all the information is with your friend. He is his own expert. The less you interfere, the more you assist him in finding himSELF.

Now you and your friend should be ready to actually start with the fourth sonance exploration. Be sure to finish it with a verbal exchange, or if you are working alone, with entries into your journal or your tape recorder. Your verbal exchange at this point should become more and more of a monologue. By now your friend is very familiar with the procedure and should be able to talk rather freely in his own way about his own experiences. They most probably include not only sensations and feelings, but also reactions to his expressive movements, and visual images.

After your friend has finished his exploration, let him be your agent and prepare yourself to go through the fourth sonance exploration.

THE KEY TO LEISURE

The problem of finding a lifestyle for tomorrow is not answered by changing from one activity to another. If you change from working to playing golf, for instance, you do not necessarily change your attitude from "work" to "play." You can only change by adopting a different lifestyle attitude.

Let me tell you a story of a golf partner of mine. He works every day in his father's business. At his office he has a high old time. He pats the secretaries' behinds and drinks coffee. But in the afternoon it is an entirely different show. He **kills** himself **playing** golf. You can see the agony in his face and almost hear the acid burning holes into his stomach. What's going on? He really likes his coffee, particularly that mountain grown stuff. He's right there with it. When he sips it, his body and his awareness are right there in one piece. How about his golf? While playing golf, walking up to the next shot, he is either reminiscing about the last five-iron (which he hacked into the ground) or he is contemplating his overall bad score and the round of drinks which he, the loser, will have to buy for all his buddies. In other words, his body walking up to the ball is separated from his awareness — which is either in the past (with the previously missed shot) or in the future (the total poor score).

A well-rounded lifestyle has a balance of spontaneity and reflectivity just as the well-functioning organism vascillates between tension and relaxation. The problem with modern living is that it is almost exclusively reflective. You constantly dabble around in your past (if my mother had only toilet-trained me later, I'd be such a better person today) or you are anxious about your future (what am I going to do tomorrow if the stock market declines?) Instead of dealing with at least half of your life in the here and now, you concern yourself almost exclusively with the future or the past, and thereby miss out on the moment. When you were a child, you were completely involved with your play, with no attention to past or future. You were with it entirely. As you grow older, you get caught in the cultural spiral and become the victim of total reflectivity. When you have spontaneity, on the other hand, you are lost within the process. Past and future are of no consequence.

Reflectivity and spontaneity make up man's lifestyle. Nowadays we read a lot about lifestyle, but basically we are talking about reflective lifestyles only. All that is changed is the activity, not the attitude. Modern man has almost completely lost touch with his spontaneity. However spontaneity is the very crux of his nature. His reflective attitude is ruled by what should be and what has been. Leisure is threatening to modern man. And most people think that by changing their activities, they will resolve their problem. But instead, they find themselves working as hard at play as they do at work. I'm sure you can think of someone who attacks his vacation in the same way he works all year. He probably races from city to city or from freeway to freeway, meeting schedules and deadlines and missing it all in the process. It is his attitude that needs to change.

In order for you to find true leisure, you must change the attitude behind your lifestyle. Your spontaneous energy is rooted deep in your very nature, your body. GEBA Therapy is a way for you to get in touch with this body energy, to explore it and to integrate it into your everyday life.

Happiness in this world, when it comes, comes incidentally.
Make it the object of pursuit, and it leads us on a wild goose chase,
     and is never attained.
Follow some other object, and very possibly we may find
     we have caught happiness without dreaming of it.

Nathaniel Hawthorne (1804—1864)

THE FIFTH WEEK

THE STANDARD ENERGY EXPLORATION

Starting with this week, I will address both you and your friend directly. Once you both have successfully completed the first four weeks, you are finished with the preliminary practices. All you have to do now is to combine the key elements of the four energy explorations into the **standard energy exploration.** From then on, you and your friend can begin to practice and to explore on your own.

During the first three weeks, you were able to make your body heavy, your center warm, and your pulse calm. These three routines were designed to assist you in relaxing your body and in preparing yourSELF to drift into the energy state. Last week you supported this "drifting" experience further by repeating "I surrender mySELF, the air is breathing me" in a mantra-like fashion. This particular practice was designed to strengthen the quality of your energy state more and more. Once you are able to reach the energy state regularly and with relative ease, you are ready to put it all together into the standard energy exploration.

The standard energy exploration is a combination of the four energy explorations you have been practicing individually during the past four weeks. There is really nothing in this sequence that you haven't experienced already. It's the combination of the four explorations together that will be new to you. Here is the standard energy exploration:

> I surrender mySELF
> my body is heavy
> my center is warm
> my pulse is calm
> the air is breathing me

> I surrender mySELF
> the air is breathing me

After going through this routine a couple of times during the fifth week, you should be able to experience all of the respective body sensations. It is, however, essential at this point that you can reach the energy state with relative ease and that you can actually feel yourSELF drifting into it deeper and deeper. When you are able to surrender yourSELF deeply enough, you are ready to explore the energy state further. There are three different groups of explorations you can practice and work with while in the energy state. I call them **area**, **intent** and **image explorations**.

The way you work with them is very simple. First, you lie down and prepare yourself for this procedure, as you have done in the energy explorations before. If you have started to do the energy explorations on your own, nothing really will change for you. In case you are still accustomed to working with an agent, it will take some practice making the transition to working alone. From my own experiences, this should not be too difficult. You might have to repeat practicing some of the earlier routines. But it won't be long before you can do them completely on your own.

Second, you present the first five lines of the standard energy exploration to yourSELF in whatever way has worked for you in the past. Like this:

> I surrender mySELF
> my body is heavy
> my center is warm
> my pulse is calm
> the air is breathing me

Third, you repeat the last two lines:

>   I surrender mySELF
>   the air is breathing me

over and over continuously until you have reached a deep enough space in your energy state. By now you have developed a feeling which will tell you when you are in deep enough. As I expressed repeatedly in the fourth week, nothing can be "explained" at this stage. You practice. You experience. You know.

Fourth, you introduce the respective area, image or intent exploration, which I explain in detail in the next pages. Repeat it over and over again until you can experience the desired sensation for a longer period of time. It is entirely up to you how long you want to stay in the energy state. The "coming out" routine is used the same way as before to terminate the entire sequence:

>   My face is cool
>   my face is nice and cool
>   my face is cool
>
>   make fists
>   open your fists
>   take a deep breath
>   stretch out
>
>   (wait 30 seconds)
>
>   open your eyes

Fifth, it is entirely up to you what you do with this experience. Share it, record it, or continue to work with it in other ways that might be interesting to you.

You should find area explorations fairly easy to work with, as you have been working with body areas for 3 weeks now. Intent explorations will be more difficult, but I include them here because they work for some people and they will open up new tools for you if you have any success with them.

Image explorations should be the easiest of all to work with since visual images are a part of everyone's experience.

AREA EXPLORATION

The word **area** refers to specific places, parts, or organs in your body. In an area exploration, you must first decide what area of your body you want to work on and what type of sensation you want to experience there. By making these two choices you design your own special area exploration. The routine should be kept short and simple and should be expressed positively. Here are a few area exploration routines that have worked for me or for my friends:

For relaxation (relief from tension):
>   my face is cool
>   my pulse is steady and calm

For menstrual cramps (also for constipation):
>   my center is warm
>   my pelvis is heavy and warm

For sleep problems (insomnia):
>   my pulse is calm
>   my body is tired and warm

For hemorrhoids (anal fissures and piles):
>   my anus is heavy
>   my anus is heavy and cool

For coughing (sometimes snoring, too):
>   my chest is warm
>   my throat is soft and cool

For asthma (hay fever):

       my eyes are cool

       my eyes are numb and cool

For tension in your jaw (resentment, anger):

       my jaw is heavy

       my neck is heavy and warm

For headaches (worry, anxiety, guilt):

       my hands are warm

       my hands are heavy and warm

Remember what I said in the beginning: Words as such are not important. What is important is what type of sensation you can create in the area you selected. This is really where the actual exploration starts for you. You will have to experiment, explore, practice, and change the words until you find the sequence that works for you. On the basis of my own experience I can give you the following guidelines.

The feeling of heaviness seems to stimulate the blood flow and to raise the core temperature in the deeper layers of your body. The feeling of warmth seems to increase peripheral blood flow and skin temperature. Coolness tends to constrict the blood vessels and decrease the blood circulation. Calmness, in general, has a slowing-down effect on the pulse.

The results you can achieve with area exploration vary from person to person. So it is up to you to spend enough time to find the "right" word combination for the situation you want to achieve. Your experience with the first four energy explorations will help you in your area explorations. Once you have a sequence that works for you, use it over a longer period of time and continue to observe yourself. Your friend, your recorded observations or your journal can be very useful feedback in area exploration work.

Area explorations can be useful at specific times. For instance, in the case of menstrual cramps or migraine you can do your explorations before you expect the pain, just at the onset of an attack or at any time during the process. Your experience will teach you when to work.

Area exploration can also be used to intensify your feeling in a specific part of your body. Here is an example:

For sensual excitement:
> my vagina is warm
> my vagina is heavy and warm

As you can see, the possibilities are nearly unlimited. Now, more than before, you will realize how much you are really engaged in **explorations**. They are all yours and only you can tell if they work for you or if they need to be adapted or changed. Go ahead. Experiment with them, and with your body.

INTENT EXPLORATION

This group of explorations makes it possible for you to change the attitude behind your activities and thereby change to a more SELF-acceptable pattern. In other words, your best intentions can be achieved if you really want them. You can give up cigarettes. You can pass up that second helping of food, that third martini, that sleeping pill. You can give up your "bad" habits and begin to change your attitude toward yourSELF. Likewise, you can begin to sustain an erection, remember your dreams, relax your body, or achieve an orgasm. You can develop "good" habits and gratifying activities. Your intentions can become reality instead of merely New Year's resolutions.

As before, the routines in intent explorations should be to the point and stated as positively as possible. Use the standard energy exploration to get into the energy state as deeply as possible and then introduce the specific intent exploration. Here are some examples:

Tension:

> My tightness is leaving me
> I am relaxed and calm

Bedwetting:

> I wake up when my bladder is heavy
> I wake up when my bladder is full

Alcoholism:

> I have stopped drinking
> I will never take another drink

Pill-popping:

> I have quit taking pills
>
> I will never take pills again

If you want to remember your dreams:

> I remember my dreams
>
> I always remember all of my dreams

If you have difficulty sustaining an erection:

> My penis is erect
>
> My penis is stiff and erect

If you have difficulty achieving an orgasm:

> I surrender mySELF
>
> I enjoy feeling my body.

Intent explorations are very flexible and can become extremely rewarding to you. On the basis of the results you get, you can change the design of your routine until you find the right way for you. You must seek the method and words which work best for you. As with the other explorations, only you will **know** what works and what doesn't. You are your own expert throughout the entire process. The responsibility is with you.

IMAGE EXPLORATION

By now you have probably discovered visual images, and might even have experimented with them. In the process of getting into the energy state, you can't help becoming aware of all kinds of colors and forms that seem to appear spontaneously before your eyes. The best way for you to start exploring visual images is by following whatever you see when you are in the energy state. Usually you first notice white, cloud-like forms. If you stay with them long enough, they might turn into ice-blue shades with their forms constantly changing. Just put your awareness on your visual images the same way you concentrate on sensations during sonance explorations. By practicing continuously, you will eventually be able to choose the colors you see, to produce any color at will. As you progress, you may be able to see yourself sitting opposite from you, look at your body from the inside, envision objects from chairs to monsters, or still forms and moving forms, concrete forms and dream-like forms.

Image explorations in themselves provide you with unlimited opportunity for further experimentation. You can do many kinds of work on yourSELF with them. For example, here are some ways my friends have used image exploration with good results:

Start out by doing the standard energy exploration to reach a deep energy state. Then introduce the respective image exploration.

Dreamwork: Introduce the final scene of a dream that you keep having but never seem to finish. Follow spontaneous images as far as they will take you. Perhaps you can complete some unfinished business.

Childhood: Introduce yourself into your visual image of the way you were at five years of age sitting on your father's lap. Lie there and watch these "image movies." You might find out some interesting things!

Obesity: See yourself very fat. Really let yourself be drowned by your fat. Then slowly let the image disappear and replace it with a slender you. See yourself dancing, twirling, leaping, moving and feeling very good — really liking yourself.

Ugliness: Allow yourself to see yourself as very ugly. Dwell in detail on all the features you dislike about yourself and then let this image disappear and replace it piece by piece, like a puzzle, with all the things you like about yourself. Change your hair and let it flow in the breeze. Give yourself the facial expression you want to have. Write your own story.

Hypertension: Visualize yourself with a big head. Then picture yourself walking out of your head into your body — into your feet, into your toes, up to your thighs, your chest, over into your arms and all the way down into your genitals.

Smoking: Start out by seeing yourself in a fit of coughing. Image your lungs, black as soot. Throw the cigarette away. Now see yourself sitting on the beach taking a deep breath and feeling good about your breathing. Start to run freely without puffing.

Insomnia: See yourself going to bed, climbing under the covers. Stretch. Aahhhhhhhhhhhhhh. Yawn and close your eyes. Watch yourself fall asleep.

Sensuality: Experience yourself really free as far as your own sensuality is concerned. See yourself opening your thighs, moving your pelvis. It's your body and you feel good. Drown yourself in explorations of your own sensuality.

You can also introduce cue words that are significant for certain situations or problems in your life which you want to explore. All you have to do is tune into these words while you are in the energy state and then follow the visual images that occur spontaneously. Here are some examples: kindergarten, freedom, intercourse, war, mother, anger, women, etc. What you experience during the image exploration might shed some new light on yourSELF. Also, keeping a record with a follow-up verbal exchange of your image exploration might be enlightening for future reference.

I know several people that like to work with their eyes open. It is more difficult to get into the energy state this way. You can practice in very much the same way you did with your eyes closed before. It is very important, however, that you "see without desire." This is the kind of seeing that allows you to just open your eyes without concentrating on anything or fragmenting your visual experience in any way.

So you can see that the world which opens up for you in image exploration lends itself to very practical applications as well as to the discovery of new and exciting horizons.

THE STANDARD SONANCE EXPLORATION

You and your friend begin the fifth week by working on a couple of supportive practices. The first one is called the **body lift**. To begin it, ask your friend to lie down on a couch in a supine position. Tell him to breathe deeply enough through his nose so that you can pick up his breathing rhythm. Then stand next to him and put your hands on his waist and slide them together behind his back until the fingers of your hands touch each other. The moment your friend begins to exhale, lift him slowly off the couch with your hands underneath his lower back. As he begins to inhale, put him down into the original

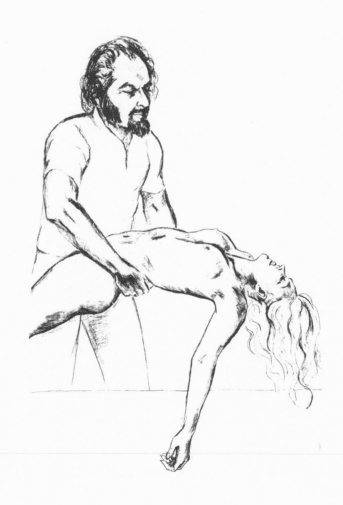

position. Lift him again the moment his exhalation begins and so on. Increase the heights of the lift gradually by raising your friend's pelvis from about six inches to two feet off the ground. During this supportive practice, your friend can experience a feeling of total surrender to himSELF.

If your friend is lying on the floor, or if he is too heavy for you to lift, there is another way of doing this practice. Straddle your friend while facing him, bend down and put your hands behind his back as I described above. Then, instead of lifting with your arms, just straighten your back and lift him by stretching your legs. This way your legs are doing the work and you can lift more weight with less effort.

Encourage your friend to yield to the pull of gravity and to let go of himSELF completely. The body lift then becomes the true emBODYment of his attitude of total surrender. If this attitude, this surrender to himSELF in the here and now, is not experienced, the open position as such has very little value. On the contrary, the direct pursuit of forcing himself to open up against his feelings will rather have the opposite effect. It will make it impossible for him to fully experience himself. Instead he continues to look for a conflict outside of himself while the real battle is taking place inside of his body. He is his conflict. I will talk more about this subject later on in the book.

There is another way for your friend to experience the attitude of "I surrender mySELF" through a supportive practice called the **leg spread**. Ask your friend to lie down on his back, to pull up his knees and to plant his feet firmly on the ground. Let him lift his pelvis several times from the floor and put his awareness into the soles of his feet. This will help him to center himself — to have contact with the ground. Now tell him to coordinate the raising of his pelvis from the floor with his inhalation. His hip reaches the highest point when he finishes breathing in. Then there is a short pause before the exhalation

160

begins. During this pause, have him concentrate on his pelvis and his thighs. Ask him to get in touch with the control he has over this part of his body. Now tell him to give up the control, to exhale and to allow his thighs and his pelvis to open up. The pause before the next

inhalation starts is the best place for him to begin to experience the attitude of surrender. This feeling can further be intensified by giving a sigh of release or pleasure while breathing out. Let him practice this movement about ten times. The leg spread is not quite as demanding as far as surrender is concerned. But you can easily sense the increased openness and vulnerability that this movement is expressing. It is advisable at this point for you to go through the same routine yourself. It will help you to gain more insight into supporting your partner. So, now change places and let your friend help you to experience the body lift, the leg spread and the surrender to yourSELF which they bring about.

Now that you and your friend are ready to be introduced to the **standard sonance exploration**, both of you are far enough along to take complete charge of your own progress. I will again talk to each of you directly as I did for the **standard energy exploration**.

When you are the explorer, you do the breathing and determine the duration, the intensity, and the content of a session by listening to your body. Otherwise there is nothing "new" about the standard sonance exploration. The "new" will spontaneously surface whenever you are ready to allow it to surface. The standard sonance exploration, like the standard energy exploration, has no rules. GEBA Therapy has no rules. It is a method of no method. **GEBA Therapy is an un-method.**

If you are the explorer, prepare yourself for the standard sonance exploration as you have done in the past. Begin to breathe when you feel you are ready to. Pay attention to sensations in your body and tune in to the areas where you can experience sonance vibrations. If you have no feelings or if you feel tight, numb, or cold in a specific body zone, tell your agent about it. He can then assist you with supportive practices in order to help you to remove your energy blocks and become sonant throughout your entire body.

If you are able to get in touch with any emotions, allow them to surface and express them through any motion that feels "right" to you. If you feel a need to talk, then talk. Talking is just another motion, another expression of the organism. Any verbal exchange following the standard sonance exploration should be initiated entirely by you, the explorer.

If you are the agent, you should be very much in the background now and should only participate directly when your friend asks you to. He is on his own. You should keep your hand on his center, providing him with unbroken sustenance. Today, and in the days ahead, introduce supportive practices strictly on the basis of what your friend reports to you. If he feels that his hands are very cold, work on his hands. If he tells you that he experiences his thorax to be stiff and tight like a drum, assist him with the chest pump. If he says he is tense between his shoulder blades, ask him to roll over on his stomach and apply the three-part back stroke. If he has no feeling in his pelvis, suggest the leg spread to him. If he informs you that he is sonant in his chest and sonant in his center but unable to connect the two zones, do the body lift. So you see, as you go along, the progress of the standard sonance exploration evolves entirely out of the explorer's experiences.

By the end of the fifth week, the sessions become more and more an intimate and personal experience. Hardly any verbal exchange takes place during the actual sonance exploration, but the verbal exchange afterwards has more importance. By doing both energy and sonance explorations, you gain deeper insight into yourSELF through the wisdom of your body. You get in touch with material and work your way through it. Your thinking and talking then is the language of your very nature.

Your value as an agent in this process of unfolding and growing is one of a good listener. You should never analyze, interpret, explain, or manipulate. By being responsible to yourSELF, you will know when and how to respond to your friend.

YOU ARE YOUR HEMORRHOIDS

Your body takes care of itself through a built-in self-regulatory mechanism. When your body needs food, it gets hungry, feeds itself, and stops eating as soon as it is satisfied. Eating is one activity in which your awareness is at the service of your organism. Your nature is taking care of things. You live spontaneously. Unfortunately, there is a way for you to interfere with this natural process of self-regulation — by handing your body over to your head (cortex). For example, instead of listening to the body clues when it is ready to eliminate, you go to the bathroom when you "think" it is a good time to go (early in the morning before breakfast, immediately after breakfast so you can rush off to work, etc.) Then you sit down and **press**. When you press, your body tells you that it is not ready to eliminate — by tightening your anus. Your body is defending its integrity against your headtrip. A very similar thing happens in everyday life when you are under stress. When you anticipate, and feel nervous tension, you hold on to your anus. Let me show you what this does to your body. Your anus is surrounded by a network of interlacing blood vessels, referred to as the anal plexus. This plexus is supplied with blood by arteries which run along the inside of the internal sphincter muscle. The vessel walls of these arteries are strong enough to withstand even the most extreme muscular contractions. This is not the case with the veins which remove the

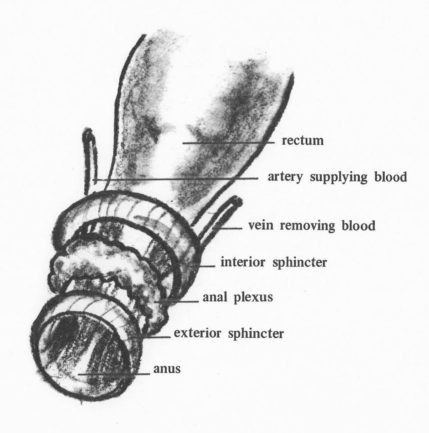

rectum

artery supplying blood

vein removing blood

interior sphincter

anal plexus

exterior sphincter

anus

blood from the plexus. If the inner ring-muscle reacts with a spasm the veins get strangled. When this happens, venous blood no longer can go under the internal sphincter muscle and the anal plexus becomes congested. The blood vessels swell and either burst eventually or get strengthened with connective tissue by the self-regulatory mechanism of the body. Your hemorrhoids are the result!

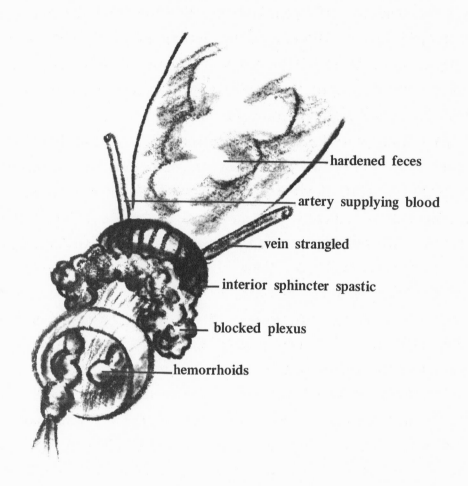

hardened feces

artery supplying blood

vein strangled

interior sphincter spastic

blocked plexus

hemorrhoids

So what you actually have here is a conflict between the body and the head. When you get hemorrhoids, you say that your body is sick. No. You **made** your body sick. You are on a headtrip; you override the message your body is sending and pay the price in the form of hemorrhoids. This "illness" is the result of the struggle of your head with your body, the result of your abortive lifestyle. You have brought about this DIS-ease yourself. Your head decides when to get up, when to go to sleep, when to eliminate, when to eat, but your body is not in agreement with this schedule, which has been worked out by your head to "fit" your abortive lifestyle. And the only way for you to get rid of this DIS-ease is by getting in touch with your body. Listen to it. Tune in to it. Put your awareness into the service of what is and not constantly into the service of what you think should be. The "shoulds" can never really become yours.

What can you do about hemorrhoids? You can have someone operate on them or you can try drugs, ointments, and suppositories. The question remains, however, whether you are really taking care of your problem or are merely treating its symptoms. I contend that you are only treating the symptoms. And these symptoms will either reoccur or other symptoms will take their place, so long as the cause remains unattended. Then what is the problem? What are those hemorrhoids? The hemorrhoids are an indication of how you live. And the **how** stands for your attitude — which makes or breaks your lifestyle. Your hemorrhoids are a sign of breaking. You **are** your hemorrhoids.

Well, how do you live? What attitude do you have behind your life? Maybe it's like this: You are running things. You have a few people to supervise. You are responsible for them. You design contacts. You feel responsible for those too. You worry about the people and the contracts. You are afraid of losing control over the situation. You wish you could do everything yourself. You can't stop thinking about it. You can't sleep. You have hemorrhoids. You are tense. You can't really relax over the week-end.

Can you see the writing on the wall? You are anticipating all the time. Your awareness is racing all over the place and your body hurts. Your suffering is real. How can you get out of this vicious cultural spiral? Through GEBA Therapy. Let me show you how:

1. Supportive Practices:

When you are at work and you have a couple of minutes available, do the following supportive practice: lie down on your back in the usual fashion, either on a couch or on the floor. Close your eyes. Put your awareness where your anus is. If this is difficult for you, just contract your anus a few times. This will help you to get a feeling for it. Now open your mouth and begin to breathe. Coordinate the inhalation with the contraction of your anus. On top of each inhalation, hold on to both your breath and your anus for a couple of seconds. During this pause, put your attention on different zones of your body. Start with your face and finish with your anus. This practice will get you in touch with the muscular tension in your body. At the end of each pause, let go of your breath and your anus. Combine each exhalation with a sigh of relief or pleasure. Put all your awareness into the general feeling of "letting go" of your anus and of releasing yourSELF.

2. Energy Explorations:

At least once a day do the standard energy exploration. Just by remaining in the energy state for a few minutes, you feel relaxed and recharged afterwards. This should also have some beneficial effect on your hemorrhoids. While in the energy state, you can introduce the following explorations:

a)   **area**

my anus is heavy
my anus is heavy and cool

b)   **intent**

I release mySELF in my anus
I am relaxed and at peace

c) **image**

> Start out by seeing yourself sitting on the floor with your knees pulled up and holding on to them very tight with your arms. Experience yourself letting go and opening up until you are lying on the floor, sprawled out and totally relaxed.

3. **Sonance Explorations:**

Go through the standard sonance exploration at least twice a week. If your hemorrhoids are really bothering you, do your breathing routine every day. Incorporate the supportive practice I just described to you at the beginning of your sonance exploration. Later on, concentrate on your pelvis and allow yourself to be sonant in your anus. During the last part of each sonance exploration, start to pay attention to your emotions. If you get in touch with a specific emotion, let it surface and express it if you feel like doing so. For example: you become aware of a "tenseness" in your jaw, you experience a "holding on" with your hands. You get in touch with a "pulling in" of your anus. You feel up-tight. You are unable to let go. You are afraid of losing control. You experience a building up of frustration. You discover a feeling of sadness. Your eyes are filling up with tears. You allow yourself to cry. Tears are streaming down your cheeks. You say over and over again: "I am sick of controlling people." Then you lie quietly and experience a sense of relief. You sense yourSELF being very much in the here and now. You are relaxed.

By practicing GEBA Therapy, you continue to experience yourSELF more and more. This process provides you with deeper insights into **how** you are living. You become aware of your Body/Awareness Split and you discover GEstalt Body-Awareness — all of this on the basis of your very own experiences. That's when you know.

4. GEstalt Body-Awareness:

Now that you **know** how you live and what kind of attitude dominates your lifestyle, you **do** something about it. You transfer your insights and experiences from your practice sessions into your every day life, by practicing what you know in actual life situations. For instance, if you catch yourSELF getting up-tight, manipulating people, or feeling angry, you listen to yourSELF and then you act. Don't think what you should do! If you feel a tremor in the body, the body is trying to tell you something by this tremor. It tells you "I am shaking." "I am angry." "I want to cry." But here comes the head. It tells you to control yourself, to not let yourself go. Don't let your feelings show. Don't cry. Pull yourself together. What will the neighbors think! You block yourSELF. You hold the lid down and in that very moment you lose the sense of your body, the feeling of yourSELF. By staying true to your nature, you liberate yourSELF and open up a new world, a world without hemorrhoids.

YOU ARE YOUR SEXUALITY

The scheduling of food intake, elimination, and sexuality is relatively new in the history of mankind. There are still people in many cultures who eat whenever their body tells them to eat. The three square meals idea is strictly the product of your head. So is the idea of connecting your sexuality to going to bed at night, propagation and a culturally-determined sexual morality. After all, the need for sexual gratification is part of your nature in the same way your need to eliminate or to eat is. Sexuality is with you from the very beginning of your existence and is expressed through movements like touching, holding, stroking and other body contacts. You experience it as pleasure, as closeness and as intimacy with others. You are your sexuality. You are your body. But you are your awareness too. It is your awareness after all, which allows you to fully experience your sexuality, by uniting it with your body. You can, however, also keep yourSELF from experiencing your sexuality by splitting your awareness from your body. When you do this you turn yourSELF off. Your body, then, is no longer the source of spontaneity and pleasure. Instead, your head takes over and manufactures its own excitement in the form of sexual headtrips. Your body becomes a mere object and your genitals become a tool of your head. Your penis or your vagina are the very extention of your brain. Your head is in charge and your body is no longer a part of this process. When this happens you no longer follow the morality of your organism, your nature. Instead of "making love" in the true sense of the word, you go through the motions only and the pay-off is in your head. Instead of losing yourSELF in the movement, you go after an ulterior motive. Sexual activities become the means to an end. You use them to prove your masculinity, to punish your partner by withholding your cooperation, to control, to pay back, to intimidate, etc. The list is endless. The general feeling which surrounds sexuality is well illustrated by the way in which words depicting intercourse are used: "Fuck you!" "I got screwed!" "She is all fucked up!" These phrases have nothing to do with love-making. They are negative expressions of hatred, resentment, and power. But, then again, what does "love-making" have to do with sexuality? Is the act itself a sign of love any more than it is a sign of hatred, resentment, and power? All of these words are the language of the head and the act itself can be made into whatever your head wants it to be. The act is neutral and your organism has its own inherent morality.

In order to rediscover your sexuality you first must rediscover your body. By uniting your awareness with your body, you free yourSELF from your headtrip. You change your attitude. You surrender yourSELF. You do not surrender to another man or another woman. Your level of sexual activity has very little to do with other people. You can be as out of contact with your sexuality by "conquering" a different girl every night as you can by denying yourself the experience completely. In both cases your head is dictating what to do and using your body as the means to an end.

You can help yourSELF to rediscover your sexuality. Let me show you how you can turn on again, by using a woman's inability to achieve an orgasm as an example.

First of all you must realize that **you are your problem.** You do have orgasmic potency but you also do have ways to control this potency. Both processes, the expression and the control of orgasmic potency, require energy. When you keep yourself from expressing yourSELF, you bind this energy. You have energy blocks. In the case of the inability to achieve an orgasm, these blocks can be very complex. Sexual gymnastics and aphrodisiacs alone are not going to do the trick. The key to reactivating your orgasmic potency is by changing your attitude and acquiring the ability to surrender yourSELF. What makes this so difficult is that surrender cannot be directly pursued, like

172

happiness cannot be directly pursued. The same is true about achieving an orgasm. You cannot go out after it. You must start out first by working on yourSELF.

1. Supportive practices:

Lie down on your back. Pull up your knees and plant your feet firmly on the ground about six inches apart. Lift your pelvis several times off the floor and put your awareness into the soles of your feet. Keep your knees slightly open and experience the contact you have with the floor in both of your legs all the way up into your pelvis. Coordinate the lifting of your pelvis with your inhalation. Then allow your thighs to open wide while your pelvis returns to the ground. Exhale during this motion with a deep sigh of pleasure. Pause a little and get in touch with the feeling of surrender before you start to inhale again. Practice this routine about twenty times every day. The movement and its rhythm will become more and more a part of you. As soon as you start to feel this way about it you are ready to introduce an additional movement. Contract your vagina during inhalation and let go of your vagina with each exhalation. Everything else remains the same.

2. Energy Explorations:

You reach the energy state only if you can allow yourSELF to surrender. In other words, if you are able to have GEstalt Body-Awareness. This is the same attitude you must have in order to experience an orgasm. Reaching the energy state helps you to practice putting your body and your awareness together. While you are in the energy state you can experiment with the following explorations:

a)   **area**

My vagina is warm
My vagina is heavy and warm

173

b) **intent**

> I surrender mySELF
>
> I enjoy feeling my body

c) **image**

> Introduce the words **surrender** and **pleasure** and see where
> your imagery leads you. Put a scene before your eyes
> which you experience as sensually and sexually arousing.
> Watch it develop.

3. **Sonance Explorations:**

Supportive practices and energy explorations prepare you.
Sonance explorations get you there. Practice the standard sonance
exploration every second day. Incorporate the supportive practices, which
you did earlier, into your sonance explorations. Later on, concentrate on
your genital zone and allow yourself to be sonant in your vagina.
During the second half of your sonance exploration, fish for your
emotions. The inability to reach an orgasm is very closely linked to
blocked feelings like resentment, guilt, or shame. Before they are
resolved, progress is almost impossible. Continue to pay attention to
yourSELF. If you get in touch with your emotions, allow them to
surface and act on them if you want to. For example: The first
sensation you might become aware of is a tightening of your mouth.
Then you get in touch with tension in your neck and your discover
yourSELF making fists. At that very moment you realize that you are
angry. You say "no." You repeat saying "no" louder and louder. You
kick the bed with your legs and pound it with your arms. Then you
stop shouting and hitting. You lie quietly and allow yourSELF the
experience of having SONANCE all through your body. You are aware
of being in the here and now with your body. You have GEBA. As you
lie quietly you discover new insights into your life.

174

4. GEstalt Body-Awareness:

You have been able to surrender yourSELF in the sheltered setting of your room. You also have integrated yourSELF by working through energy blocks. Now you begin the more difficult task of expressing the energy that has become available to you through your sexuality. Don't push it. Stay in touch with yourSELF. You will know when the time is right. If you don't achieve an orgasm, it is all right. Just concentrate on experiencing the pleasure of your body. Forget about the orgasm. Enjoy every moment of your experiences. The orgasm will happen when you no longer expect it to happen.

There is no Good, there is no Bad
These are the whims of mortal will
That works me weal, that I call good
What harms and hurts I hold ill
They change with place, they shift with race
And, in the veriest span of time
Each good was banned as Sin or Crime
Each faith is false, all Faith is true
Truth is the shattered mirror strewn
In myriad bits, while each believes
His little bit the whole to own . . .
Thy faith, why false? My faith, why true?
Tis all the work of Mine,
Only the foolish love of self
Makes the Mine excel the Thine.

Haji Abdu l-Yezdi
(translated by Sir Richard Burton)

THE BREATHING CYCLE

Through breathing you connect yourSELF with the spontaneity of life. You are being breathed before you do the breathing. Behind your breathing is the same kind of intelligence that turns a caterpillar into a butterfly. The more you control yourSELF with your head, the more you interfere with the spontaneity of your breath.

If you are suddenly surprised or scared, you immediately suck in air and hold on to it. This is a spontaneous reaction of your organism. Your breathing is interrupted just long enough to prepare your body for flight or attack. Once you start moving, you continue to breathe. It is a different story when your head takes over. Your body keeps reacting to worries and fears which your head thinks up. You cannot attack your head nor can you run away from it. This way you keep yourSELF in a state of anxiety and tension for a lifetime. You are stuck. You keep holding on to the air. It makes your feel tense, powerful, and in control. Or you are scared to let go of the air. Then you feel threatened, depressed, and without energy. In both instances you control yourSELF.

In order to be able to give up the control of your head you have to come down into your body by letting go of the air first. You have to allow yourSELF to breathe out. When you exhale, you discharge energy and you experience a feeling of release. When you inhale, on the other hand, you charge yourself with energy and experience a feeling of control. Living and growing takes place in the interchange of these polarities. They are in appearance two, but in essence one. Alone they are nothing. They only hang you up on either end of your breathing cycle. Either you turn yourSELF over to the control and power of your head (headtrip) or you lose yourSELF in the release and pleasure of your body (energy state). You miss out on yourSELF if you spend your life in either extreme.

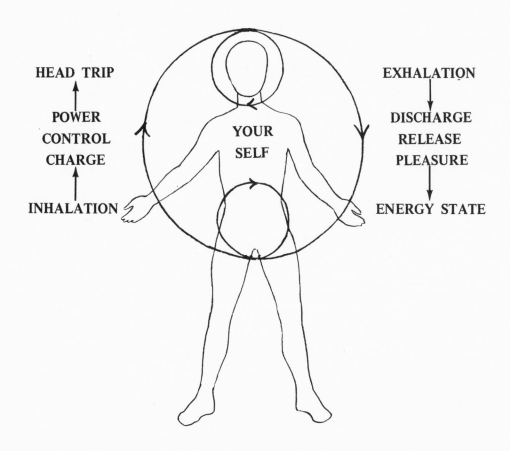

Through GEBA Therapy, you rediscover your natural breathing cycle by tuning in to your body. Your inhalation and your exhalation, your changing and your discharging, your reflectivity and your spontaneity all operate under the same principle as the Chinese **Yang** and **Yin** or the Indian **Shiva** and **Sakti**. What goes up, must come down. Without it there is no movement, no change, and therefore no growth.

Let me show you how this wheel of growth concept works:

1. You hold on to your breath. You are in control or you are scared to let go. You anticipate and you reminisce. You breathe shallow or

hardly at all. **You reflect yourSELF**. You are in your head. **You have reflectivity.**

2. Supportive practices help you to get in touch with your level of tension. You let go of your breath. You experience how you feel when **you release yourSELF**. You discover the interplay between tension and relaxation. You **have tonicity**.

3. Supportive practices also make you aware of your manner of carriage. You experience how you feel when your posture and your movements are in harmony with the forces of gravity. **You center yourSELF**. You breathe out completely. You are grounded. **You have contact.**

4. Energy explorations show you how to shift your awareness. You are between breathing out and breathing in. **You surrender yourSELF** to this moment. You are in the energy state. **You have spontaneity.**

5. Sonance Explorations help you to rediscover the quality of your breathing. You start to breathe in. **You integrate yourSELF** by working through energy blocks. Energy becomes available to you. **You have sonance**.

6. Now that you have energy available for living and are free of tension, **you liberate yourSELF**. Your breathing in gives you more energy. You live spontaneously. You have GEstalt Body-Awareness.

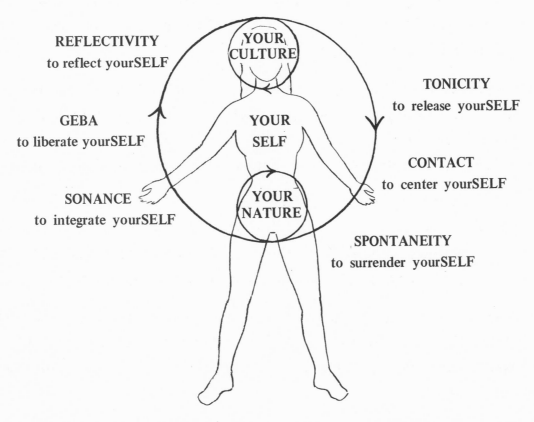

REFLECTIVITY
to reflect yourSELF

YOUR
CULTURE

TONICITY
to release yourSELF

GEBA
to liberate yourSELF

YOUR
SELF

CONTACT
to center yourSELF

SONANCE
to integrate yourSELF

YOUR
NATURE

SPONTANEITY
to surrender yourSELF

As soon as your reflectivity participates in the wheel of change, it becomes an essential part of your lifestyle cycle. By reflecting what you experience, you add another dimension to your life. You create, you anticipate, your reminisce, but you don't get stuck in your head any longer. You know how and when to release, to center, to surrender, to integrate, and to liberate yourSELF. The cycle is complete. In its continued motion lies the key to growth and health. Let go of yourSELF. Live dangerously. Introduce GEstalt Body-Awareness into your daily life.

This is the end of the book. I hope it is the beginning of an exciting life with less tension and with plenty of spontaneous energy available to you for more healthful living and emotional growth!

REFLECTIVITY is the way of the BODY
the body is the way of the EARTH
the earth is the way of NATURE
nature is the way of SPONTANEITY

AN INTERVIEW WITH BRUNO
by Jean Porter

Jean: Bruno, most therapies center around the body or around the psyche. But the type of therapy that you do seems to combine both body and psyche into an entity that cannot be divided. When did you first make this connection, this non-duality of body and awareness, as you call it?

Bruno: Well, of course, it didn't happen all at once. It goes all the way back into my high school days in Vienna. When I was in classical secondary school one of my professors was an extremely fascinating man and looking back, I think it was through him that I got interested in biology, psychology, and sports.

Jean: What did you do after high school?

Bruno: I finished high school shortly after World War Two and enrolled in the National Institute of Physical Culture in Vienna. It was there that I was introduced to different movement systems, methods of massage and manipulation, and to the therapy and pathology of breathing. The first realization of the importance of the body-awareness entity came with one of the jobs I had. I worked with amputees using various rehabilitative techniques and preparing them for the fitting of their protheses. But I soon found out that their problems were not only physical in nature. Their wounds had healed well and they had learned how to use their artificial limbs. Their real problem was their inability to face life again. As I worked with them we talked; this is when the real therapy started. From this experience, for the first time, I recognized the importance of direct body contact and personal intimacy when working on problems of living.

Through my work with amputees I also became familiarized with the so-called "phantom limb phenomenon," which has to do with imagined sensations in the area where the amputated limb used to be. At that time two Viennese physicians, Paul Schilder and Otto Poetzl, did extensive research in this field and it was through them that I was introduced to body image phenomena and to Dr. Oscar Vogt's "prophylactic autohypnosis." My own energy explorations originated from these ideas.

Jean: After the Institute of Physical Culture where did your interests take you?

Bruno: Well, after that, I worked with juvenile delinquents. It was then that I realized how tremendously important physical activities are when dealing with young people. My experience with touch, movement, and the use of other non-verbal methods as therapeutic tools goes back to those days.

Jean: Of course, you have had a great deal of formal education too.

Bruno: Yes, but I always made it a point never to let my studies interfere with my education. I entered a doctoral program at the University of Vienna and this is where I became familiar with existentialism, phenomenology, Gestalt psychology, and a variety of therapeutic systems.

Jean: Then you spent your entire early life in Vienna and were deeply influenced by the current trends in that particular center?

Bruno: Yes, this is true. On the whole, post-war Vienna definitely had the greatest impact on my life. You see, during the War the work of many great Viennese thinkers was suppressed because of their political or religious convictions. Right after the War, all of this work surfaced and it was very exciting to discover everything new again.

Jean: Sigmund Freud was one of those people, wasn't he?

Bruno: Yes, Freud being Jewish had to leave Austria to avoid persecution.

Jean: You mean that during the War all of this work lay in state until after the War when it errupted onto the scene with new impact? It was like a rebirth.

Bruno: Right. We started to dig up books that had been forbidden and began to contact people who were familiar with suppressed theories and methods. This is how I personally became introduced to the therapy of Wilhelm Reich and his concepts on sexuality and energy flow.

Jean: After your studies at the University of Vienna, where did you go?

Bruno: I accepted an interesting offer from the Ministry of Health and Education in Iran and spent three years in Teheran as an advisor. My duties included teaching and lecturing and I had extensive opportunities to travel. It was there that I became interested in Eastern philosophies and religions and in Sufi poetry.

Jean: I think of Iran as a gateway to the East. Is this where you got first-hand experience with methods of meditation and breathing?

Bruno: Yes. As a matter of fact I experimented extensively with autohypnosis and breathing systems of Indian origin. The formulation of the basic concepts for the sonance explorations go back to those days.

Jean: After your three years in Iran, where did you go?

Bruno: I returned to Vienna and received an offer from the Chicago industrialist, Walter Paepcke, to come to the United States and help in the development and operation of the Aspen Institute for Humanistic Studies. I became the director of the Health Center of the new Institute which was, in my opinion, the first "growth center" in the United

States. In the humanistic tradition, the Institute reintroduced the concept of the whole man. We had music and art festivals, discussion groups, recreational activities, and therapy. It was a very exciting place for me to live and I met many interesting people there with whom I'm still in contact.

Jean: Aspen certainly is one of the ski capitals of the world. Have you done a lot of skiing in your life?

Bruno: Oh definitely. Skiing has been a part of my life since I was three years old. In Aspen during the early season, I always spent time helping to train the U.S. Olympic team and with members of the International Professional Ski Racers Association.

Jean: How long did you live in Aspen?

Bruno: I stayed there for over six years. Then after the death of Walter Paepcke, I left Aspen, and moved to Albuquerque where I accepted a position at the University of New Mexico. The University allocated the time for me to work at the Lovelance Foundation for Medical Education and Research. It was there that I was introduced to Dr. Perls "Gestalt Therapy." I also assisted in several research projects in physiology and finished my thesis for an American doctorate from the University of Colorado.

Jean: Well, you certainly have done a lot of traveling.

Bruno: Yes, after four years in Albuquerque I got married and my wife and I sailed around the world with the University of the Seven Seas, an ocean liner. After this experience, we decided to settle in California. I was particularly attracted by the San Francisco Bay Area. Its avant-garde climate and sophistication reminded me very much of my native Vienna.

Jean: It was in San Francisco that you first began lecturing and conducting your own private practice, wasn't it?

Bruno: Yes, I started to teach for the California State University system in San Francisco and in Sonoma, for the California School of Professional Psychology, and was for a time associated with the Institute for Multiple Psychotherapy. We bought a home in Marin County where I opened my private practice and where I still live with my wife, Suzanne, and our two sons, Dorian and Peter.

Jean: Tell me, what do you like to do in your spare time, Bruno?

Bruno: I like to play golf. So does my wife and even my two little boys have started to swing the clubs. We all love to ski and head up to the Sierras whenever we find time.

Jean: How did you get started on this book?

Bruno: It was through one of my therapy workshops that I met Don Gerrard, the editor of this book, and his wife, Eugenia. They both became interested in my work and asked me to write about it. We decided to write the book as practical and direct as possible. It was very challenging to me to use an analytic tool like the written word in trying to capture the feeling of very personal experiences.

Jean: Your book certainly has met this challenge. Tell me how you plan to use your book in conjunction with your private practice.

Bruno: Before individuals meet with me, the book can give them a general introduction into the methods of GEstalt Body-Awareness Therapy. Through the book the reader can get an impression of me as a person and can gain some insight into my philosophy of healing. At the first session, I always present a copy of the book to each person I work with.

Once a person is in therapy with me, the book definitely serves as a handbook and reference manual. For instance, it contains the exact wording of the energy explorations. The book, of course, is nothing without your own experience!

Jean: What can a person do after going through the five week program in the book?

Bruno: Don't forget, you're not working on the book! The book is only giving you a tool to assist you in working on yourself. Once you have the tool, you can go on forever. We're never finished working on ourselves. There is always room for growth.

Jean: Do you consider any time after five weeks as advanced work?

Bruno: Here again, it depends entirely on the individual. You cannot put this type of work on a value scale. What is advanced for one person is self-evident for someone else. People throughout their lives are in different places at different times and are bothered by different problems of living. The book provides the reader with a method, but what is really important takes place in the experience of the individual. In this respect, the horizons of this book are unlimited. Everything a person does is strictly intuitive and spontaneous and I am sure that some people will carry these methods further than you and I can imagine.

Jean: What value do you see in sharing the experiences of GEBA Therapy with another person?

Bruno: My therapy is not different from other experiences in life. If you go to the movies alone, it is a much less fulfilling experience than if you had gone with your friend. The "agent" concept is based on this sharing and growing together — with the realization, of course, that you have to do your growing up yourself.

Jean: Will you be available for consultation and training?

Bruno: Yes, I will continue to offer workshops, to teach, and to give lectures and demonstrations throughout the United States and Europe. And, of course, I will maintain my private practice, which is very important to me.

Jean: Do you plan to write other books in the near future?

Bruno: Yes. I have made sketches on a book about movement and emotions. Also, I have many notes on what you might put under the heading of "Preventive Psychiatry." The emphasis is on liberation through self-knowledge and the exploration of lifestyles rather than on treatment and cure. For me, the struggle is **for** health rather than **against** disease. And any method aiming at personal growth and healthful living cannot exclude the body. These principles will be the guiding themes of the book.

Jean: How did you happen to meet Roselyn, the illustrator of the book?

Bruno: We put an advertisement in several newspapers and interviewed about forty people. Roselyn's powerful and sensitive style appealed to me most and she was chosen to illustrate the book.

Jean: Do you know where she received her training?

Bruno: Yes, at the Harris School of Advertising Art in Nashville, Tennessee, and at the Academy of Art College in San Francisco.

Jean: If anyone who reads your book would like to get in touch with you or Roselyn, how can they contact you?

Bruno: By writing to: The Bookworks
1409 Fifth Street
Berkeley, California   94710